17.95

Paranormal Planet
Files of the Paranormal Intelligence Agency

Jack Cary

MAR 23 2021

Ms. D. R. Toi

_A 23602

www.paranormal-intelligence-agency.com

ISBN: 978-0-359-569137

Contents

Chapter 7
The Abduction of Bigfoot? The Link Between Sasquatch and E.T.'s

Chapter 8
The Antarctica Enigma

Chapter 1

The Unified Field Theory of Paranormal Activity

"Any sufficiently advanced science will be indistinguishable
from magic."
-Arthur C. Clark

For a very long time now, I have suspected that underlying
the vast amount of different types of paranormal activity being
reported to us and to other investigators, was a pattern of
evidence to connect them all to a singular source. The pieces of
this puzzle are vast and wide ranging in scope. When they are
placed together, however, they present a breathtaking whole.

Many of my readers are aware of the Cattle Mutilation
phenomenon or as I refer to it, the Unexplained Animal Death
Phenomenon. This was very much brought to the attention of the
American public by way of the work of the renowned researcher
Linda Moulton Howe. What is so interesting about the Cattle
Mutilation phenomenon is that this occurrence is not limited to
cattle but to almost every animal one can think of. The fact that
this is the case and that victims of this phenomenon stretch from
wild lizards all the way up to humans, and that this occurs in
every country around the world, indicates to us that any and all
theories whereby these activities are being conducted by some
sort of, as yet, undiscovered and unnamed black operations
military group, are in error.

A very close examination of a vast amount of ancillary evidence running parallel to this phenomenon indicates to me that this phenomenon, in its entirety, casts a shocking light on what might be the singular source of this and many other paranormal mysteries happening around the world.

Cat's, Cattle and Chronic Wasting Disease:

Many readers are aware of the phenomenon known as cattle mutilation but have not seen nor heard the evidence for this phenomenon happening to both a vast amount of varying animal species and, most shockingly, to humans. For a long time, the cattle mutilation phenomenon was being presented by the key investigators into this mystery, as an occurrence that only happened to the cattle species. In the course of those key investigations, however, several other types of mutilated animals with matching wounds to those found on cattle were also reported and investigated. Now we have a highly credible body of cases of this occurring to a vast number of biological species around the world. In some of the most recent occurrences, wild lizards were discovered with perfect dissection wounds and organs surgically removed. In recent years, human cases of this phenomenon have also been discovered.

Charles Fort reported a number of these cases occurring in the late 19th and early 20th century in England. In America the earliest documented accounts came from Kansas and Pennsylvania, however, the first case of this to gain national attention occurred in 1967 in the San Luis Valley of Colorado.

An organization known as the National Institute for Discovery Science, which is funded by billionaire Robert Bigelow, conducted an extensive multi-year study of the cattle mutilation phenomenon and published their findings in a scientific paper titled 'Unexplained Cattle Deaths and the Emergence of a Transmissible Spongiform Encephalopathy (TSE) Epidemic in North America'. This organization employs some of the finest scientists in the world to study various phenomenon of a paranormal nature and this study of theirs is both extremely well investigated and presented.

Key to their findings are the following points of consideration. The paper states:

"Overall, the evidence suggests that animal mutilations are a long-term, covert, prion disease sampling operation by unknown perpetrators who are aware of a substantial contamination of the beef and venison food supply. Although this paper presents evidence in favor of a motive for animal mutilations, there is still insufficient evidence to identify the perpetrators."

"The hypotheses described in this paper yield a number of testable predictions. Examining these predictions in the coming months and years is increasingly urgent because they have considerable public health implications. Secondly, the recent

(May 2003) announcement of a case of mad-cow disease in Alberta, Canada has brought the issue of the contamination of the human food chain into sharper focus."

The abstract of the NIDS paper and its bullet points of immediate concern are as follows:

"We present evidence that a correlation exists between reports of animal mutilation and the emergence of a Transmissible Spongiform Encephalopathy (TSE) epidemic in North America."

* *"We show that sharp instruments are used in animal mutilations. Our data contradicts the conclusions of the 1980 Rommel Report that claimed predators and scavengers could explain reports of cattle mutilation."*

* *"Using data obtained from a NIDS nationwide survey of bovine veterinarian practitioners, we show that certain organs are preferentially removed during animal mutilations."*

* *"We focus attention on the temporal and geographical overlaps between the animal mutilation and TSE epidemics in NE Colorado. The most highly publicized TSE epidemic in North America, chronic wasting disease (CWD), emerged in NE Colorado in the late 1960's."*

* *"We show evidence that patterns of animal mutilations conform to covert but classical wildlife sampling methodologies for infectious diseases."*

* *"We show evidence in support of an epidemic of prion disease that is both sub-clinical in cattle and clinical in deer/elk in North America."*

The one question not satisfactorily answered by NIDS's efforts at solving this mystery is that they were unable to obtain enough information to ascertain who was perpetrating the clandestine testing of our food supply. That is the question I hope to answer as it is placed within a larger context of paranormal happenings and ancillary evidence.

What is even more fascinating about this mystery is that the testing program moved on to house cats. In August of 1989 the New York Times wrote an article about the finding of 67 cats mutilated in Tustin, California. The New York Times article states:

"Some of the cats were cut in half with what some say is almost surgical precision, others disemboweled or skinned. One resident said, 'There is never any blood at the scene, the animals are often dismembered with surgical precision and paws and other body parts are often left on the ground in strikingly similar

arrangements. No one ever seems to hear anything, nor do dogs bark during the killing.' It was believed the cats were captured, taken elsewhere, their blood drained and organs removed, then replaced on their owners' lawns."

(I have included the photo of the sheep mutilation to show the similarity between the wounds.)

In March of 1993, Linda Moultan Howe and Dr. John Altschuler of Denver, Colorado obtained a specimen of one of these cats from a wave of mutilations taking place in Alberta, Canada. Upon microscopic examination it was determined that the entire excision was made by an instrument with a very high heat source. The above photo is of that specimen. The wound was caused and simultaneously cauterized by the same instrument. Notice in this case, like so many others, that the stomach and its contents have been removed.

Waves of mutilations of house cats have occurred since the 1970's and sometimes other small animals are found as well. Animals found with these wounds include rabbits, squirrels, marmots, lizards, dogs, raccoon, and rats. These waves have been documented in the U.S., Canada, and the U.K. They occur cyclically every few years and the following cities have had the most occurrences:

Wheat Ridge, Colorado
Denver, Colorado
Aurora, Colorado

London, England
Vancouver, Canada
Toronto, Canada
Tucson, Arizona
San Antonio, Plano, Ft. Worth, Austin and Corpus Christie,
Texas
Seattle, Spokane, Washington
Falls Church, Virginia
Palmetto Bay, Cutler Bay, Pensacola, Navarre, Lauderhill,
Florida
Lee, New York
Tucson, Arizona
Tustin, San Jose and San Diego, California
Salt Lake City, Utah
Oklahoma City, Oklahoma

Here again, in the case of the half cat mutilations when we look deeper, we find the probable motive for them being tested for prion proteins. In the case of the cattle, the scenario plays out like this. When certain black budget scientists working for the U.S. government began testing Kuru Virus on our country's native wildlife population, and one of the specimens escaped from a testing facility in Ft. Collins, Colorado, they inadvertently compromised the North American beef supply. This occurs because deer and elk do not pay attention to barbed wire fences and hop right over them as though they aren't even there. Once they have gained access to the grazing grounds of our cattle populations, they feed off the plants leaving infected saliva deposits behind. The cattle then feed off the same plants and become infected with the virus. The virus shows up in cattle as Mad Cow disease and in humans as Jacob Creutzfeldt Disease and other prion protein maladies. The NIDS has presented compelling evidence that these prion protein diseases are being mis-diagnosed in the human population as early Alzheimer's disease. In the case of house cats, when we began to dig deeper we discovered a rather shocking fact. House cats are the most invasive species ever introduced into the North American continent or to any continent around the world. In a recent scientific study chronicled by Nature.com we find the following critical information.

The biologists who worked on the new study pored over research culled over the past several years to estimate how many cats live in the US, and what their killing habits might be. They estimate that roughly 84 million owned cats live in the US, and that there are 30-80 million un-owned cats, which include feral cats, barn cats, and cats who are not allowed inside. The researchers "estimate that free-ranging domestic cats kill 1.4–3.7 billion birds and 6.9–20.7 billion mammals annually." They emphasize that "un-owned cats" are the culprits here. Though the numbers may be shocking, their discovery isn't particularly startling. Un-owned cats have already been implicated in 33 modern bird, mammal, and reptile extinctions, write the researchers in *Nature Communications*. They continue, the major scourges for wildlife were not those free-ranging, owned-cats, but instead feral and un-owned cats that survive on the streets. Each of those kitties - and the team estimates between 30 million and 80 million of them live in the United States - kills between 23 and 46 birds a year, and between 129 and 338 small mammals

These facts indicate to the PIA that the perpetrators of this unlawful testing program are quite concerned that the prion protein infestation has now spread to the wild bird population. In the case of the cattle and other wildlife like deer and elk the concern is that they have become infected through contact with one another and sharing the same grazing territory. In the case of the cats, they are concerned that the birds they are eating have also become widely infected. This is also the case with the small mammals being found with the same wounds. The house cats are also responsible for the killing a vast number of small mammals every year.

Let us turn our attention to the perpetrators and their possible motives because therein lies the real focus of this chapter as it relates to a unified field theory of paranormal activity. I now identified two separate but likely related sources that I believe can account for the vast majority, if not all, of the paranormal happenings taking place across our planet.

I also believe that it is through the intricate investigation of the Unexplained Animal Death or Cattle Mutilation mystery that a serious and most disturbing insight can be gleaned as to the possible implications of this being the case. When we examine the history of the Cattle Mutilation phenomenon, it is interesting to note that the first widely reported case of this occurring in America was to a horse named Lady in the San Luis Valley of Colorado in 1967.

Photograph of first documented case of cattle mutilation.

An interesting note to this case is that Nellie Lewis, the owner of the horse became increasingly obsessed with UFO's in the months following the mysterious death of her horse. She eventually committed suicide at the base of Mt. Blanca. Days after her death a group of volunteers showed up to her home to help clean out all her belongings. Nellie Lewis was known to have kept a diary of her experiences with UFO's in the San Luis Valley. The day the volunteers showed up so did two unidentified men who volunteered to help. Shortly after these strange men left the home, it was discovered that Nellie Lewis's diary was also missing.

I investigated a very similar case in recent years, and I believe that on this occasion the perpetrators left a clue never seen in any of the cases. In fact, it just might be the best evidence ever collected in the UAD/Cattle Mutilation mystery. On November 9, 2013 Terry Mcilvaine of Fairview, Tennessee discovered that his Palo Fino horse had suffered the same fate as so many Cattle, Cats and other mammals before him. What was different about this case is that Terry Mcilvaine had two infrared security cameras in his field watching over his horses and we believe that those cameras caught our very first glimpses of the perpetrators of this testing program. More shockingly than that is the evidence that we will present that this testing program is in fact being conducted by a so-called Type II or Type III civilization and that the earth and its inhabitants are playing an unknown role in this civilization without their knowledge.

In the Mcilvaine case on two separate dates and times days before the mutilation occurred the following photographs were obtained by infrared security cameras.

Notice that the horse does not react at all to the light source which indicates to us that the source is completely silent. This is the first and only time that anyone has captured a picture of the actual perpetrators of the cattle/U.A.D. mystery.

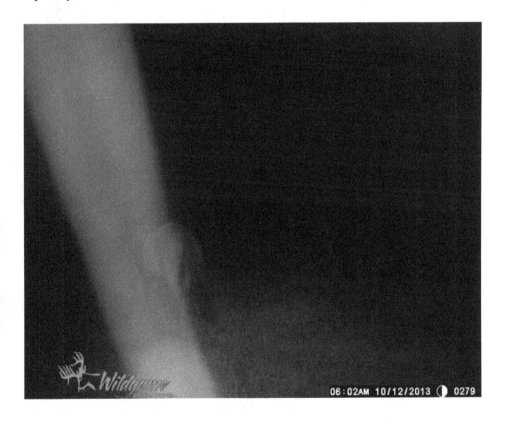

06:02AM 10/12/2013 (0279

Whatever the source of this light, it did not spook the horses and it returned on two separate occasions prior to the killing

and sampling of the horses. No one noticed any strange beams of light in the area leading us to believe that this was an Infrared light source and that the camera's night vision capability was able to catch the light beam.

This photograph is the best photograph ever taken of the perpetrators of the U.A.D. phenomenon. Whatever intelligence is behind the bright source of light in this photograph is the same intelligence behind this very scary and very sad phenomenon. Whatever was the source of the light, it carefully

chose these animals beforehand and detected the cameras in the field rendering them inoperable on the night of the mutilations.

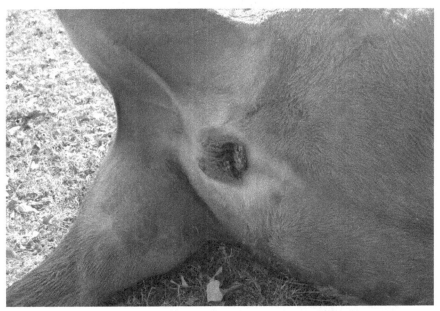

If readers are unfamiliar with the concept of a Type II or Type III civilization, then the following information will be useful.

The **Kardashev scale** is a method of measuring a civilization's level of technological advancement, based on the amount of energy a civilization can harness and therefore use for expansion. The scale has three designated categories called *Type I*, *II*, and *III*. A Type I civilization – also called planetary civilization– is able to utilize and store energy available from its neighboring star which reaches their planet, Type II is able to harness the energy of the entire star (the most popular hypothetic concept being the Dyson Sphere—a device which would encompass the entire star and transfer its energy to the planet), and Type III civilization are in control of energy on the scale of their entire host galaxy. The scale is hypothetical and regards energy consumption on a cosmic scale. It was first proposed in 1964 by the Soviet astronomer Nickolai Kardeshev. Various extensions of the scale have been proposed since, from a wider range of power levels (types 0, IV and V) to the use of metrics other than pure power.

The Kardashev scale allows for a Type III civilization and this could very well be the case regarding the earth and my Unified Field Theory of Paranormal Activity. As Arthur C. Clarke once stated, "Any sufficiently advanced technology is indistinguishable from magic." What we believe we are witnessing is exactly that, technology so advanced that it often appears indistinguishable from magic and that its source is a Type II or Type III civilization which is monitoring this planet and the human species down to the D.N.A. level. Many readers have heard of the so-called Drake equation proposed by Frank Drake the inventor of the radio telescope. This is the equation he developed to theoretically calculate the number of advanced civilizations possibly surviving in our galaxy.

Frank Drake.

The Drake equation is:
$$N = R_* \cdot f_p \cdot n_e \cdot f_\ell \cdot f_i \cdot f_c \cdot L$$
where:
N = the number of civilizations in our galaxy with which communication might be possible (i.e. which are on our current past light cone);
and
R_* = the average rate of star formation in our galaxy
fp = the fraction of those stars that have planets
ne = the average number of planets that can potentially support life per star that has planets
fl = the fraction of planets that could support life that actually develop life at some point
fi = the fraction of planets with life that actually go on to develop intelligent life (civilizations)
fc = the fraction of civilizations that develop a technology that releases detectable signs of their existence into space
L = the length of time for which such civilizations release detectable signals into space
  This gave Enrico Fermi, the Italian physicist the impetus to create his 'Fermi's Paradox'. This is an equation with the idea that according to the Drake equation, there should have been a civilization already in the Milky Way galaxy that had achieved a type II or type III designation as it would only
take approximately a million years of technological advancement for such a feat to be possible by any given intelligent civilization. Fermi, who developed the world's first

nuclear reactor, noted that there are billions of stars in the Milky Way galaxy and if this was the case then:

- There are billions of stars in the galaxy that are like the Sun, many of which are billions of years older than Earth.
- With high probability, some of these stars will have Earth-like planets, and if the Earth is typical, some might develop intelligent life.
- Some of these civilizations might develop interstellar space travel, a step the Earth is investigating now.
- Even at the slow pace of currently envisioned interstellar travel, the Milky Way galaxy could be completely traversed in about a million years.

According to this line of thinking, the Earth should have already been visited by extraterrestrial aliens. In an informal conversation, Fermi noted no convincing evidence of this, leading him to ask, "Where is everybody? "There have been many attempts to explain the Fermi paradox, primarily suggesting either that intelligent extraterrestrial life is extremely rare or proposing reasons that such civilizations have not contacted or visited Earth.

What Fermi didn't count on in his speculations is that the earth and its inhabitants were somehow a part of a vast galactic civilization that must fit the type II or type III Kardashev hypothesis. We have examined the animal mutilation phenomenon, but the human species is also being examined on an ongoing basis, apparently by the same civilization that is responsible for the animal mutilation phenomenon. I have also found very disturbing evidence of human mutilation cases and these don't even reflect the very real problem of 'alien abduction' which we believe to also be part of the type II, III agenda of this still unidentified master civilization. One such case is the human mutilation case of Guarapiranga, Brazil.

This case is the one case I consider to be the most disturbing of all time because of the coroner's observations and conclusions upon post-mortem examination. Notice in the coroner's photographs the similarity of wounds to the victim that are found time and again on cattle mutilations. The coroner observed in his official notes that whatever caused the wounds on this victim was a machine and most disturbing of all, he believed the machine had been designed in order perform that specific function and no other. In other words, this was done by a type of machine that was designed and manufactured to cause those exact wounds on a human. The victim was drained of blood in identical fashion to other animal mutilations.

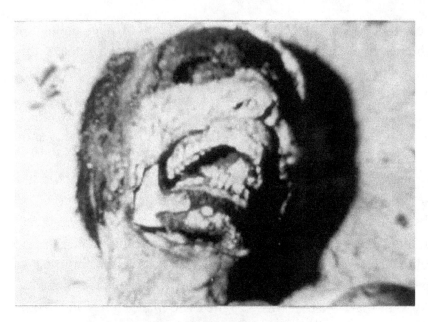

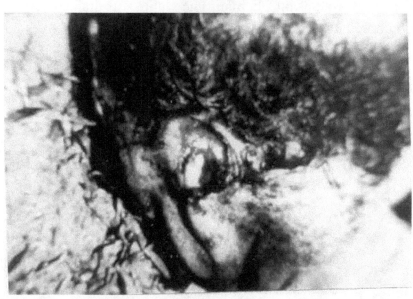

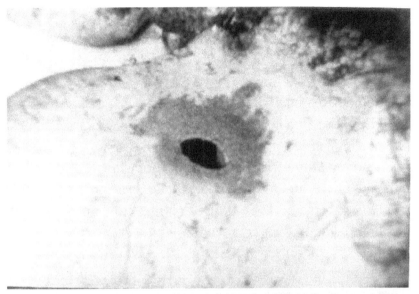

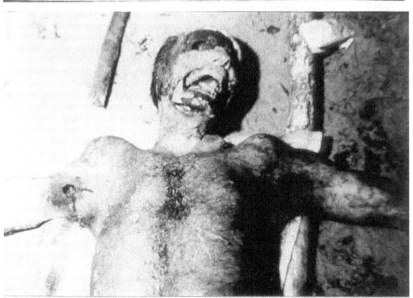

In short, the coroner believed this individual was both alive and paralyzed when these wounds were inflicted and that he died from "vital reaction". In other words, he died from the pain being inflicted to him while he was still alive.

Intrepid researchers into the Alien Abduction phenomenon like Dr. David M. Jacobs and the late Dr. John E. Mack, Bud Hopkins, and Whitley Strieber, have amassed an amazing body of evidence regarding this disturbing phenomenon. I believe that human abductions and the subsequent genetic sampling, is being conducted by the same Type II or III civilization that is conducting the animal and human mutilation cases.

What is further interesting about the Alien Abduction phenomenon is that we believe the reported 'grey' alien types who are most often reported in these cases, to be a type of biological robot that is somehow programmed to perform that function and no other. The technology is so advanced that just like the Arthur C. Clarke quote that opens this book, it appears to us like magic. As Clarke stated, "Any sufficiently advanced science will be indistinguishable from magic." This has led some to believe that the cattle mutilation phenomenon must be spiritually malevolent activity, but this is simply because the technology is so advanced that only a type II or III civilization would be able to develop it.

In many animal mutilation cases, there is direct physical evidence that the animal was dropped from a very great height. Often cattle found with these wounds have shattered rib cages on the underside of the animal where the carcass has impacted the earth. In other cases, the perpetrators drop the animal not realizing that the animal could end up like the deer in the following photograph. The deer in the photograph was found on this power line pole in a rural area outside of Eugene, Oregon. The dog in the other photograph below was found hanging from a remote power line in New Mexico. Other cases have included a myriad of land animals found in the tops of trees.

Bloodless animal mutilation with laser like cuts

In many these cases, circumstances surrounding the event preclude human involvement and seem as if they occur almost by magic. One such case is featured in the NIDS report referenced in this article. In this cattle mutilation case, the event occurred in broad daylight within 300 yards of the ranchers who owned the property and who were in the field branding new born calves. They did not hear or see anything that day even as the calf they had just branded was butchered a mere 300 yards from them in broad daylight. The mother of the calf was found limping nearby with a broken leg. below is a photo of the actual calf as it was found that day. It appears to have been consumed from the top down.

It is my contention that these acts are being performed by a technology which is not dissimilar to our unmanned drones. We believe there is overwhelming evidence to show that only a technology that could have been developed by a Type II or Type III civilization could be possible for such acts and the fact that it is being done at all much less on a planetary wide scale makes only a couple of probabilities viable. The expense and time investment in conducting such a long running and large-scale operation lends us to conclude that we are in fact playing a role in this unknown and willingly clandestine civilization. We can only either be a genetic experiment of some to kind to achieve an unknown end or we reside within a type of nature preserve which is the property of this unknown Type II/III civilization. When we examine the now famous Majestic 12 documents leaked to Ryan and Bob Wood in 1996, we find a document titled Top Secret Ultra Interplanetary Phenomenon Unit Summary Intelligence Assessment. This document is from the War Dept and dated July 22, 1947 and states:

*"The most disturbing aspect of this investigation was that there were **other bodies found not far from Landing Zone 1 that looked as though they had been dissected as you would a frog.** It is not known if Army field surgeons had performed exploratory surgery on these bodies. **Animal parts were reportedly discovered inside the craft at Landing Zone 2** but this cannot be confirmed. The team has reserved judgement on this issue."*

In a recent breakthrough an invention of a new kind of telescope was invented that reportedly allows the user to see U.F.O. craft, which are invisible to the naked eye. This scientific paper was published in the American Journal of Modern Physics and can be found on our daily intel report page (http://www.paranormal-intelligence-agency.com/apps/blog/show/43764783-american-journal-of-modern-physics-reports-evidence-of-u-f-o-s-using-new-type-of-telescope) In short, the paper states that this new type of telescope was invented to detect antimatter particles and as a side effect the inventor discovered that he was witnessing U.F.O. craft in various orbits who are apparently using antimatter as a propulsion fuel and that these craft were expelling anti-matter particles which renders them invisible to the naked eye. This is just the newest piece of a very complex and disturbing puzzle which in totality is pointing us to a singular conclusion

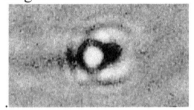

Photo of one of the unknown crafts detected by new telescope technology.

I believe there is plenty of credible evidence to show that a very large percentage of activity which is reported as being paranormal in nature is, in fact, the byproduct of our interaction with a Type II/III civilization which has gone to great expense to not only conceal their presence from us, but also to what appears to be a very long running program of environmental testing on all levels from our D.N.A. to the food supply we consume and so on. Paranormal activity covered under this interaction would include:

Animal Mutilation Phenomenon

Alien Abduction phenomenon and the resulting implants or tracking devices

All credible U.F.O. sightings and close encounter episodes

Ancient unexplained structures and historical anomalies of all kinds

Space structure anomalies like the structures found on both the Moon and Mars

Simultaneous Bigfoot/U.F.O. sightings (These creatures are being abducted for their D.N.A. study as well.)

Missing persons clusters in both urban and rural areas such as the National Park System

The other body of paranormal activity can be explained as inter-dimensional in nature and is facilitated by the third principle of the Mach effect which allows for the natural formation of benign wormholes. These wormholes are generated in areas where the topography allows for certain magnetic fields to be generated. The vast body of all paranormal activity including the sightings of certain crypto-zoological creatures can be accounted for under one or both source points. I believe that interaction between this planet and a Type II/III civilization and/or inter-dimensional activity facilitated by the Mach effect can account for the totality of paranormal happenings occurring on this planet.

Chapter 2

Missing 411, The Mach Effect, And Parallel Dimensions

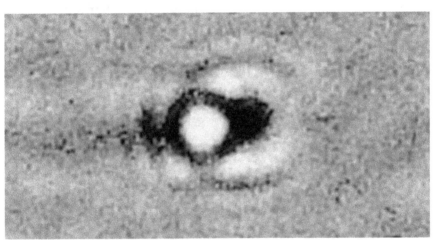

Photograph of U.F.O. taken through new telescope that picks up traces of antimatter.

In the last few years a researcher and former law enforcement officer named David Paulides has garnered widespread attention for his investigations into the abnormally large number of missing persons cases in America's National Park system. Paulides has performed an exhaustive investigation into these disappearances and has been able to find very valuable patterns and similarities in many of these cases. I have now examined these patterns and similarities in detail and have developed my own working theory to explain the cause of this disturbing phenomenon.

Upon careful analysis of the known facts of Paulides highlighted cases, I began to realize that there could, in fact, be a scientific explanation for this disturbing phenomenon and I was reminded that the paranormal is the normal, just not yet understood by man. In my unified theory of paranormal activity this would fall under the interdimensional branch. My theory combines a known scientific theory called the 'Mach Effect' with known geological science and theoretical physics to help provide a possible explanation to the Missing 411 phenomenon.

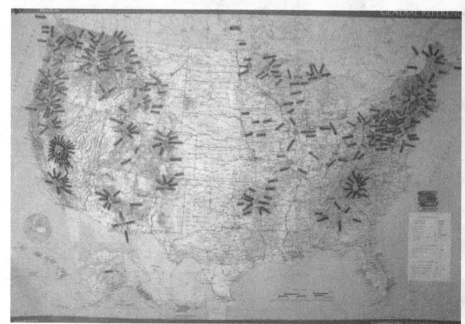

Cluster map of missing people in the National Park System.

Many theories have been proposed to explain this phenomenon from Sasquatch abductions to E.T. activity and even more exotic explanations. None of these proposed theories fits with the known facts of the individual cases themselves. In recent days a new Missing 411 case has been opened. This involves a young man from Cleveland, Ohio on vacation in Southern Colorado. This missing individual disappeared while taking a simple jog while on vacation in southern Colorado. No trace of him was found despite exhaustive efforts by search and rescue teams. Eventually his body was recovered.

This case fits perfectly with the rest of the Missing 411 phenomenon. All the details surrounding his disappearance are nearly identical to other cases.

Around the world in hushed conferences and in published scientific journals some of the best physicists alive today are attempting to relate current physics theories to observed anomalies or paranormal phenomena. Basically, their scientific musings and wandering equations are beginning to sniff out the possibility that at least some reported paranormal phenomena could be the result of inter-dimensional beings or time travelers accessing our space time continuum. Likewise, they are posing the possibility that physical beings jumping across vast distances of space via wormholes or stargates as a possibility for some UFO activity.

One hair raising variation of the interdimensional hypothesis posits that creatures or beings that access our physical reality need not be physical but may be capable of influencing our physical reality and could be capable of such acts as mind control. Some have theorized that they could manifest their influence through long term evolutionary manipulation and act as an unseen influence on human affairs. It could be that any perceived motive would be entirely incomprehensible to us in a human sense.

Some renowned scientists, like Michio Kaku, are beginning to realize what may be a grim reality for the human species. Kaku writes, "Let's say that a ten-lane superhighway is being built next to an anthill. The question is: would the ants even know what a ten-lane super highway is, or what it's used for, or how to communicate with the workers who are just feet away? And the answer is no...if there is another civilization in our backyard, in the Milky Way Galaxy, would we even know its presence? There's a good chance that we, like ants in the anthill, would not understand or be able to make sense of a ten-lane superhighway next door."

This view is shared by other leading physicist like Beatrice Gato-Rivera who have begun to embrace what their science and intuition are telling them and who have begun to ask questions unthinkable in academia only a few years ago. Gato-Rivera wrote, "If there exist thousands, or millions of parallel universes, separated from ours through extra-dimensions it would be natural then to expect that some proportion of these universes would have the same laws of physics as ours and many of the corresponding advanced civilizations would master the techniques to travel or 'jump' through the extra dimensions. This opens up enormous possibilities."

The question now being debated among these scientists is whether someone 'out there' in a parallel dimension or from far away points in time and space could get here and interact with our reality in bizarre ways. Michio Kaku suggests, "Aliens may be here now, in another dimension, a millimeter away from our own." Kaku is careful to point out that wave frequencies of other dimensions, times and universes are all around us every moment of every day. He states; "However just like you can only tune into one radio channel, you can only tune into one reality channel, and that is the channel that you exist in. The catch is that we cannot communicate with them, we cannot enter these universes." Kaku and his colleagues agree, however, that far more advanced beings could possess the technological capability to make the jump between dimensions or parallel universes. Other scientists from disciplines unrelated to physics are surprisingly converging on the same conclusion.

The late Harvard psychiatrist Dr. John Mack won a Pulitzer Prize for his book on the alien abduction phenomenon. He came to believe that there was a connection between all manner of paranormal activity. He wrote; "Taken together, these phenomena tell us many things about ourselves and the universe that challenge the dominant materialist paradigm. They reveal that our understanding of reality is extremely limited, the cosmos is more mysterious than we have imagined, there are other intelligences all about some of which seem able to reach us. Consciousness itself may be the primary creative force of the universe, and our knowledge of the physical properties of this world is far from complete. The emerging picture is a cosmos that is an interconnected harmonic web, vibrating with creativity and intelligence, in which separateness is an illusion."

What these scientists don't yet realize however, is that the 'vortex' areas are doorways between dimensions. They believe according to their science that the doorways could and should be there and yet haven't accepted the reality that the doorways are there. The bizarre and bewildering events at these sites represents nothing less than a physical interaction between dimensions. At each of these sites one finds very strange electromagnetic energy fields. Physicists believe that other dimensions are very real and that it is entirely possible that beings exist in those dimensions. They also believe that the only thing separating dimensions is an electromagnetic membrane. What is occurring at these vortex sites is that the unusual electromagnetic energies at these sites caused by the underlying geology causes a thinning or opening in the membrane allowing for momentary or intermittent interaction between our dimension and others.

This is something the United States Military must be aware of and must consider a threat in some manner, how else can we explain their presence at each location as well as their desire to buy up the land on which these sites now rest? It is though they have posted a guard at each of the 'doors' to monitor the activity and to somehow perhaps combat it. The wide array of parallel and differing paranormal activity reported at these sites fits perfectly with what these scientists describe an interaction of this sort would be like.

In one of Paulides newest books regarding the Missing 411 phenomenon, he focuses on the fact that many of the cases have occurred in areas that possess so called 'Devil Names'. These areas include names like 'Devil's Den', 'Devil's Lake', 'Devil's Canyon', 'Mt. Diablo', etc. This fact struck a major chord with our research and is identical to the research of one of the world's most renown cryptozoologist, named Loren Coleman.

In Coleman's well researched book 'Mysterious America', he discusses the fact that many types of paranormal activity are always associated with places that have historical 'Devil' names and that, in fact, these places all earned their names because of the observed paranormal activity by the local populations who in times past equated it with the work of the Devil. In Appendix 5 of Coleman's 'Mysterious America' one can find a complete list of these names and places as well as the observed paranormal activity. This fact and the fact that many of the missing 411 cases also have occurred in these same areas is far too much of a coincidence for me to accept as random possibility. In December of 2014 Paulides was interviewed on Veritas radio and stated that a new pattern seems to have emerged with his research. This new revelation is that at the same time that some of the people vanished, he also discovered that there had been either vanishing airplanes or ships that had occurred that same day in the Bermuda Triangle. This fact almost guarantees that what we are dealing with is an interdimensional bleed through in areas that have underlying geographic topography which produce strong electromagnetic fields. My theory is thus:

The Woodward effect, also referred to as a Mach effect, one of at least three predicted Mach effects, is part of a hypothesis proposed by James F. Woodward in 1990. The hypothesis states that transient mass fluctuations arise in any object that absorbs internal energy while undergoing a proper acceleration. Harnessing this effect could generate a thrust, which Woodward and others claim to measure in various experiments. If proven to exist, the Woodward effect could be used in the design of spacecraft engines of a field propulsion engine that would not have to expel matter to accelerate. Such an engine, called a Mach effect thruster (MET), would be a breakthrough in space travel. So far, no conclusive proof of the existence of this effect has been presented. Experiments to confirm and utilize this effect by Woodward and others continue.

According to Woodward, there are at least three Mach effects theoretically possible: vectored impulse thrust, open curvature of spacetime, and closed curvature of spacetime. The first effect, the Woodward effect, is the minimal energy effect of the hypothesis. The Woodward effect is focused primarily on proving the hypothesis and providing the basis of a Mach effect impulse thruster. In the first of three general Mach effects for propulsion or transport, the Woodward effect is an impulse effect usable for in-orbit satellite station keeping, spacecraft reaction control systems, or at best, thrust within the solar system. The second and third effects are open and closed spacetime effects. Open curved spacetime effects can be applied in a field generation system to produce warp fields. Closed curve spacetime effects would be part of a field generation system to generate wormholes.

The third Mach effect is a closed curve spacetime effect or closed time like curve called a benign wormhole. Closed curve space is generally known as a wormhole or black hole. Prompted by Carl Sagan for the scientific basis of wormhole transport in the movie Contact, Kip Thorne developed the theory of benign wormholes. The generation, stability and traffic control of transport through a benign wormhole is only theoretical at present.

This is important because the Earth is also experiencing 'Transient Mass Fluctuations', as it travels through space, this in turn is causing stress in the underlying rock strata in various geographical areas where there are an unusual number of missing persons cases. This rock strata contains very large deposits of quartz crystal, which when stressed causes the generation of very strong Electromagnetic fields. These fields are 'activated' at different times and places depending on external space/time factors which produce the Mach effect. When these fields are generated then they can cause a 'benign wormhole' to form allowing for travel between dimensions. It is our contention that not only are the wide array of paranormal activity associated with these areas the result of momentary interaction between dimensions but that the high number of missing persons cases so eloquently researched by Paulides can also be attributed to this scientific mechanism. The book 'Hunt for the Skin walker' holds many important clues in this line of research and we at the P.I.A. believe that we could, in fact, be witnessing something developing, which is far, far more disturbing once the Macro implications of these findings are contemplated.

Recent cases have emerged that seem to fit perfectly with my 'Mach Effect' theory.

A new bizarre case of a missing skier in New York who turned up outside of Sacramento California with no memory of how he came to be there. He was found stumbling around still dressed in his ski gear.

The Mach Effect Theory proposes that through a natural mechanism known as the Mach Effect, benign wormholes can and do open on the Earth's surface allowing for travel between two points in time and space. The skier has no memory of how he arrived in California and had left his car, his I.D. and his passport behind at the resort.

Skier who disappeared in New York and reappeared in California.

This planet is harboring a great secret. Something extremely strange and perhaps threatening to all of humanity is beginning to play itself out. Occultists, paranormal researchers, U.F.O. investigators, the U.S. Military, Intelligence agencies and the world's greatest physicists are all converging on a singular, revolutionary point of discovery. In the United States and around the world there are specific geographic areas which harbor a disturbing secret.

In recent years very credible, professional investigators and scientists have begun to discover and document certain locations where the resident population is experiencing a wide array of paranormal activity all confined within a relatively small geographic area. The witnesses to these phenomena are almost always well respected, well established citizens who have no history of mental illness or fantasy prone episodes. In many instances the phenomena have been reported by police and military personnel who are trained observers and in almost all cases the witness does not seek to profit and or garnish any undue attention.

Paranormal and U.F.O investigators now use the term 'vortex area' to discern these specific locations. In the United States a number of these locations have now been identified. The following list is made up of locations where the most intensive investigations are now underway: Hudson River Valley, New York Ohio River Valley Sedona, Arizona Dulce, New Mexico San Luis Valley, Colorado Uintah Basin, Utah Yakima, Washington. Every one of these vortex areas is considered sacred or holy by the indigenous Native American population and all have monuments or shrines built upon them.

These are all areas which have a long rich history of magic/witchcraft practices.

Each of these areas has non-stop and ongoing paranormal and U.F.O activity often stretching back to the earliest historical records of the area. Most of the locations are on or near Indian reservations or is already government owned land or land the government is currently attempting to purchase. There is always a military presence at or near these areas. Each of these areas has extreme electromagnetic field anomalies. These anomalies can be seen by studying the aeromagnetic maps of each of the locations listed.

Phenomena reported at these sites include U.F.O sightings, sightings of black unmarked military helicopters, bizarre unexplained animal and sometimes human mutilations, poltergeist activity, sightings of unknown or 'cryptid' animals, reports of alien abduction phenomena, ghost lights, orbs, evidence of magic practices and an anomalous number of missing persons.

What is so very strange about these sites is that they don't just exhibit one or two of the phenomena listed but all of them simultaneously and with no known or yet discovered connection other than the geographic area where they are reported. One of these sites now identified as a vortex area is Sedona, Arizona which is a place of ongoing high strangeness.

During a two-year period in the early 1990's a family named Bradshaw experienced a horrifying series of unusual events. The family's trouble began with frequent sightings of orbs of light in the nighttime sky over their ranch and quickly progressed to haunting poltergeist activity followed by extremely traumatic sasquatch encounters on their property, sightings of Grey aliens, encounters with a being that appeared to have the ability to 'cloak' itself in invisibility, mutilation of both livestock and dogs and the formation of what looked like a portal of light. They reported seeing what looked like an alternate landscape through the portal of light. All of this was seen, documented and witnessed by visitors to the ranch as well as the family itself. An independent and well respected U.F.O investigator named Tom Dongo was present at the ranch during many of these episodes and was able to photograph and document many of them. The culmination of these events resulted in the book 'Merging Dimensions' which chronicles these bizarre happenings.

Sedona has long been a place held sacred by the Native American tribes who have resided in the area since antiquity. They hold the belief that Sedona is a place where the 'veil' between worlds is thin. What is interesting is that aero-magnetic maps of the region show that the mountains of Sedona have a magnetic field which is five hundred percent stronger than the surrounding countryside. According to all known U.F.O sighting statistics, Sedona has more U.F.O sightings per capita than anywhere else in the world. After the bizarre occurrences on the Bradshaw ranch the family put the land up for sale.

The land was quickly purchased by the U.S. Government, who now has a secret installation on the land and has now restricted all public access to the property. Linda Bradshaw and Tom Dongo concluded that there are rips or doors in the fabric of reality and that these doors are merging points between different dimensions and different realities.

While the bizarre occurrences were unfolding on the Bradshaw Ranch another ranching family located in the Uintah Basin of Utah began to have their own series of baffling experiences. The Sherman family purchased their ranch in the

Uintah Basin in hopes of starting a new life in the beauty and solitude of the American West. Instead of solace what they discovered was a brutal non-stop assault of paranormal activity and intrusion in their lives of alternate realities.

What they experienced was eerily like the events then unfolding at the Bradshaw ranch. They experienced phenomena of orbs and floating lights, U.F.O sightings, a black triangular craft resembling an F117 Stealth fighter with the ability to hover motionless and noiseless twenty feet off the ground, unexplained animal sightings including wolves that would vanish into thin air and also seemed impervious to bullets fired at them, weird crop markings, unexplainable cattle and dog deaths including a bizarre incident whereby a newly branded calf was butchered in less than forty minutes in broad daylight and within sight of ranch personnel.

No one saw anything and no one heard anything that day even though they never went beyond three hundred yards of the animal! When they returned to release the branded calf, they found it mutilated beyond all recognition, the head and splayed out legs being all that was left as though the animal had been eaten from the top down. The mother of the calf was found hobbling nearby with a broken leg. Bizarrely one of the greatest remote viewers still alive today would later be given this incident to view. He reported that some sort of robotic drone was responsible and that it had originated in another dimension!

The Sherman family also reported seeing a portal of light and a ghostly landscape shimmering through the opening just like the Bradshaw family in Sedona, Arizona. The Sherman family eventually sold their ranch to an organization identified as the National Institute of Discovery Science which was founded by billionaire Robert Bigelow.

Robert Bigelow is one of the more enigmatic figures involved in funding paranormal research. In his youth he experienced paranormal phenomena and decided in adulthood to spend some of his considerable wealth funding hard core scientific research into paranormal activity. He founded the NIDS and hired a team of world class research scientists to study the on-going events at the Sherman family ranch. The result of their revolutionary investigation which continues even today is chronicled in the book 'Hunt for the Skinwalker'.

The team discovered a long running tradition among the Ute Indian tribe which inhabit the region of a curse that had been placed upon them and that land by so called Navajo Skinwalker witches. The Indians in the area call the place where the ranch is situated 'the path of the Skinwalker'. Their tradition speaks of paranormal happenings on that land that go back hundreds of years and originated as a dispute between the Navajo and Ute tribes.

In the American southwest Skinwalkers are considered serious business. Skinwalkers are said to be powerful witches capable of the ability to shape-shift into various animal forms. Each of the southwestern tribe's Navajo, Hopi, Ute and other tribes each have their own version of the Skinwalker witch tradition. The American southwest is rife with tales of these witches. One New Mexico educator of these stories wrote "The Navajo Skinwalkers use mind control to make their victims do things to hurt themselves and even end their lives.

The Skinwalker is a very powerful witch. It can run faster than a car and can even jump mesa cliffs without any effort at all." According to University of Nevada-Las Vegas anthropologist Dan Benyshak, who specializes in Native American tribes of the southwest, "Skinwalkers are purely evil in intent...the general view is that Skinwalkers do all sorts of terrible things, they make people sick, they commit murders. They are grave robbers and necrophiliacs. They are greedy and evil people who must kill a sibling or other relative to be initiated as a Skinwalker. They supposedly can turn into were animals and travel in supernatural ways." David Zimmerman an anthropologist with the Navajo Nation Historic Preservation Dept. states that, "Skinwalkers are folks who possess knowledge of medicine both practical and spiritual and they are both wrapped in ways that are nearly impossible to untangle."

The Navajo or Dine' Indians are very secretive about Skinwalkers and consider information regarding them to be proprietary and not to be shared outside the tribe. There have been, however, certain Native American writers who have provided a rare glimpse into this tradition.

One Navajo writer explained, "They curse people and cause great suffering and death. At night their eyes glow red like hot coals. It is said that if you see the face of a naagloshii (Skinwalker) they must kill you. If you see one and know who it is, they will die. If you see them and you don't know them, they must kill you to keep you from finding out who they. They use a mixture that some call corpse powder, which they blow into your face. Your tongue turns black and you go into convulsions and you eventually die. They are known to use evil spirits in their ceremonies.

The Dine' (Navajo) have learned ways to protect themselves against this evil and one has to always be on guard." Traditionally Skinwalkers are said to prey only on Native Americans but in recent years this pattern seems to have changed and Anglo's are also being targeted along these tribal lands which so often skirt the so-called vortex areas. One such incident was reported by a New Mexico Highway Patrol officer. While patrolling a stretch of highway south of Gallup, New Mexico he had two separate encounters with a ghostly creature that seemingly could move fast enough to keep up with his patrol car, running alongside grinning and hissing at him. During his first encounter he said the figure appeared to be wearing a ghostly mask as it kept pace with his patrol car and the car was moving at a very high rate of speed. A few days later the officer had a nearly identical experience. Not long after the second incident a fellow highway patrolman confided in him of having seen the same specter while on patrol. This officer still patrols the same stretch of highway but is terrified every time he enters the area.

One Caucasian family reported how in 1983 while driving at night along route 163 through the massive Navajo reservation, they had the sudden sensation that someone was following them. They reported that as their truck slowed to round a sharp bend, the atmosphere seemed charged like static electricity and their sense of time seemed to slow down. Suddenly a figure lunged at their vehicle from a roadside ditch.

They described the figure like this, "It was black and hairy and was eye level with the cab." One witness recalled, "Whatever this thing was, it wore a man's clothes. It had on a white and blue checked shirt and long pants. Its arms were raised over its head, almost touching the top of the cab. It looked like a hairy man or a hairy animal in man's clothing, but it didn't look like an ape or anything like that. Its eyes were yellow, and its mouth was open." The frightened family did not stop but continued speeding down the highway in state of shock. The father was a two-tour veteran of Vietnam but was horrified by what he had witnessed.

A few days later at their home in Flagstaff, Arizona, the family awoke to the sounds of loud drumming. When they looked outside, they saw the dark figures of three men outside their fence. The shadowy figures appeared to attempt to scale the fence to enter the property but seemed inexplicably unable to do so. After their apparent failed attempt to cross the property boundary the men began to chant in the darkness as the horrified family huddled inside.

One of the patterns of these vortex areas is the so called Native American connection. At each of these North American vortex sites one finds a long running tradition of Native American witchcraft practices and the Skinwalker ranch or Sherman family ranch investigated by the NIDS is no different. In fact, the Native Americans who inhabit the area hold the tradition that the Skinwalker presence on the ranch extended back fifteen generations. The Navajo and Ute tribes have had a long history of conflict and the Ute's were known to abduct Navajo's and sell them into the existing slave trade. Because of many perceived transgressions the Ute's believe that the Navajo put a curse on them and ever since that time the Ute claim the Skinwalker curse has plagued their people.

The ranch property has been declared off limits to tribe members because they say it lies "in the path of the Skinwalker." NIDS members came to understand that this term was a catch-all phrase used by the Indians to denote a wide array of paranormal activity that they witnessed and chronicled while conducting their investigation. The scientists of the NIDS research team witnessed an amazing array of extremely disturbing phenomena and it is believed that they are continuing their work on the ranch in secret to dissuade weekend UFO hunters from crowding the area.

Other vortex areas that exhibit this same pattern of activity include Dulce, New Mexico and Yakima, Washington where the resident populations have long been victimized by a host of paranormal occurrences very similar to Sedona and the Uintah Basin.

Where I reside in Colorado is perhaps the strangest of all the North American vortex sites. The San Luis Valley has been called the 'Disneyland of the paranormal' and has had a documented bizarre history of events that simply defy explanation. One of the most perplexing and strangest of all paranormal events are the so called UAD (unexplained animal deaths) or cattle mutilations.

This phenomenon first began in 1967 in the San Luis Valley and continues to this very day. This phenomenon is now global, and it is estimated that over 20,000 head of cattle have now died under identical and extremely mysterious circumstances in the Unites States alone. The animal mutilation phenomenon has been the target of two separate F.B.I. investigations and many law officers, especially in the American southwest consider it to be the greatest unsolved serial crime in the history of the United States.

The San Luis Valley is the largest alpine valley in the world. It is eighty miles long and fifty miles wide and is rimmed with majestic fourteen-thousand-foot mountain peaks that look prehistoric in appearance. The floor of the valley rests seventy-five hundred feet above sea level. The valley has been the site of hundreds upon hundreds of UFO sightings and easily ranks as one of the most intense UFO hotspots on the planet. Mount Blanca, the fourth highest peak in Colorado dominates the valley.

The valley's paranormal legacy stretches back into the mists of time. The first Spanish explorers to the valley reported seeing strange flying lights and hearing powerful humming noises which to them seemed to come from underground. Exactly like the other North American vortex sites there is a strong Native American magic connection to the valley. The Yuma culture thrived in the valley five thousand years before the birth of Christ. The Tewa Indians who are descended from the pueblo people believe the San Luis Valley is the equivalent to the Garden of Eden. The Tewa people hold the belief that the first humans to enter this world crawled up through a hole in the ground to escape their previous plane of existence. This spot is believed to be in the San Luis Valley. They believe that they literally crossed into this dimension in order to escape an unspecified 'evil' or enemy.

The Native Americans who live in the valley today believe that the 'Creator' still lives in the mountains of the valley and that he sometimes appears to humans in the form of Bigfoot. The Navajo and Ute tribes also have a deep connection to the valley. The Navajo are known to have inhabited the valley for hundreds of years. Historians believe the Navajo were finally ousted by none other than the Ute's. The Navajo regard the valley as their most sacred space and fundamental to their culture. Mt. Blanca is known to the Navajo as Tsisnaasjini, the 'sacred mountain of the east'. It is revered as one of the four mountains chosen by the 'Creator' as a boundary for the Navajo world.

The oral tradition of these people speaks of how 'rock crystal boy' and 'rock crystal girl' reside within Mt. Blanca. The oral traditions of the South American native tribes speak of how they were once in possession of thirteen crystal skulls which they regarded as their most sacred objects. At least one of these original thirteen skulls has been discovered by the late Anna Mitchell Hedges and has undergone sophisticated testing and analysis by Hewlett Packard scientists who are the premier quartz crystal experts in the world. These scientists were awe struck by the object and one of them concluded after careful analysis that the skull should not even exist as it would be nearly impossible to duplicate using today's sophisticated technology.

Recently archaeologists have discovered macaw feathers in ancient southwestern Indian burial sites indicating that these tribes had open trade with their southern neighbors. These southwestern U.S. tribes likewise have oral traditions of having once been in possession of crystal skulls and I believe two of these skulls to have been deposited by the Navajo on their holiest mountain, Mt. Blanca. These skulls are priceless and extremely powerful, and their origins may be far stranger than anyone presupposes.

Just like the other vortex areas the San Luis Valley has a distinct military presence nearby including the La Veta Military Operations Area which according to paper work filed under the auspicious name 'Project Shining Mountain', allows the military to fly super-secret aircraft just over the eastern mountain range of the valley. Besides known military installations very near the valley, it is also believed by credible researchers that a super-secret underground military installation rests just on the southern border of the valley near the Colorado, New Mexico border and close to the Chama Canyon area. This area not surprisingly has been the site of ongoing UFO sightings and animal mutilations including one bizarre episode in the 1970's whereby a deputy sheriff who also owned a ranch in the area lost seventy-five head of cattle in just a few weeks' time.

Just like every other vortex site the valley possesses an extremely strange electromagnetic anomaly. The valley contains both minimum and maximum intensity zones near one another. The area where these fields interact is often the area where bizarre and disturbing occurrences are reported. Strangely a part of this area has sand dunes which are seven hundred feet high and which rest at the base of majestic snow-covered mountain peaks. Scientists are at a loss to explain the formation of these dunes, but they are considered a national monument and are often the site of paranormal activity.

In the course of my own paranormal investigations I often travel to the San Luis Valley and one evening, accompanied by two friends, I had my own encounter with the bizarre. On one field operation to the valley to document some of the activity reported there on nearly a daily basis, me and my companions had a run in with something that we are at a loss to explain.

One of my friends owns a cabin in the valley where we stay when we travel there and one night after arriving there and dropping off some of our gear, we decided to make our way to one of the many unusual landmarks in the valley. This landmark which overlooks the Great Dunes is a ziggurat constructed by Buddhist monks who have a monastery in the valley.

As we approached the remote ziggurat in my friend's four-wheel drive truck, we noticed movement to the left side of the road just up a small bend. As we looked, we saw a figure of what appeared to be a man scurry down onto and across the dirt track of a road and onto the right side of the road. "There's a man running across the road up there." I said to my friends who also acknowledged that they had seen him. The figure wore a floppy wide brim hat that covered their face and a checkered long sleeve shirt and dark overalls or pants. From the time the figure crossed the road till we should have come upon them was only a mere few seconds and yet as we drove up the very slight incline where this person should have been standing, there was absolutely nothing.

The reader should understand that this is a high desert plain with no trees or structures to hide behind. Looking out over a vast flat desert prairie there was no one. I saw no movement as I scanned from right to left and back again. "You've got to be fucking kidding me!" I exclaimed. My friends were equally perplexed and disturbed by what was unfolding. When I first saw the figure, I thought nothing of it only that as we drove up the small incline there would be a few cars and maybe some site seers. This structure, however, is extremely remote and can only be approached by extremely tough terrain requiring a four-wheel drive.

There were no cars parked anywhere and a cold chill slowly made its way up my spine as I realized that whoever it was, we saw either up and vanished into thin air or else were somehow hiding from us. Either prospect was a bit unsettling and it occurred to me that if they did somehow scurry down a hole or something to hide from us then they were going to have a very long walk back to civilization in an area which is literally pitch black at night and filled with grown cactus. It was right at twilight the 'in between time' when we approached the ziggurat and saw the figure. Totally bewildered, I and my friends made our way to the top of the fifty-foot-high ziggurat that overlooks the desolate desert landscape all around.

We had approximately forty-five minutes of light left at that time. I scanned the surrounding countryside until darkness took over. I never saw any movement at all and neither did my colleagues. If that was a human who had decided to somehow conceal them self from us then they were going to have a very long, very spooky, walk back to anywhere in pitch black darkness, and in some seriously daunting terrain, and yet, it was either this or the figure simply vanished into thin air. Maybe it was a Skinwalker?

There was a slight chill in the high-country air that night as we drove back to the cabin. Peering out into the vast desolate darkness to the hovering snow-covered peaks beyond I realized that I might be looking at a landscape with doorways to other times and other dimensions.

Chapter 3

The Two Most Disturbing Cases in Paranormal Research: Dyatlov Pass Incident and The Guarapiranga, Brazil Human Mutilation Case.

In my many years of research there are two cases which even today haunt me as the most disturbing ever to be documented. The first occurred in Russia in the 1950's and is known as the Dyatlov Pass Incident. The second is a real human mutilation case that occurred in Brazil and is known as the Guarapiranga human mutilation case. These stand out as the most disturbing because of the graphic nature of the wounds discovered on the victims of both cases.

In the Dyatlov Pass case eight experienced mountaineers including one ski instructor, three engineers, and seven students from the former Ural Polytechnic Institute were found dead in the most bizarre way. One team member was struck ill the night before the team was due to leave and was forced to stay behind. These now eight individuals boarded a train on January 25, 1959 in the town of Sverdlosvk on their way to a strenuous cross-country ski expedition to the Otorton mountain range located in the northern Urals.

   The team never arrived at their destination and they were never seen alive again. When they did not contact family and friends on Feb. 11 as scheduled from their destination of the town of Vizhai friends and family became concerned and demanded that search parties be deployed to locate the missing nine people. On Feb. 25th a military pilot who was part of the search party first spotted something strange on the mountainside. The next day ground searchers were able to make their way up to the abandoned encampment located on the eastern slope of a mountain listed only as 1079. Strangely enough the Mansi tribesman of the area refer to this mountain as the 'Mountain of the Dead'.

As the rescue team approached the tent, they discovered something very disturbing. The tent had been halfway torn down with snow on top of it. The back of the tent had been cut open from the inside and there were footprints from at least eight different people radiating out in all directions from the tent. The tent was empty but contained all the parties' gear and shoes. The footprints in the snow were of bare or socked footprints and a in one case, a single shoe.

Two sets of the prints led down a slope 1500 feet and to a heavily forested area. Rescue team members followed the prints till they came to a large pine tree and discovered both the remnants of a fire as well as the frozen and naked remains of two members of the missing party. Team members Doroshenko and Krivonischenko were found wearing only their underwear and had apparently attempted to start a fire while still being well within range of their tent.

Investigators noted that limbs of the tree above them had been snapped off up to 15 feet and bark samples showed human skin from the two dead men embedded in it indicating the two attempted to scramble up the tree in a panicked state. Compounding the mystery was the fact that the two bodies appeared to have been untouched.

The corpse of Dyatlov the team's leader and the man for whom the Pass is now named was found 900 feet away from the first two corpses and somewhat closer to the tent. He was clutching a small birch branch in one hand and attempting to protect his head from some unknown assailant with his other. Not far from the tent another team member Rustem Slobodin was found dead and half buried in the snow. His skull was found to have a seven-inch fracture on the back; however, his death was determined to be hypothermia. The carcass of Zinaida Kolmogorov was found furthest from the tent. There was blood around her corpse, but they could not determine if it was hers. The rest of the missing members were not discovered till Spring some 225 yards down a ravine from the two corpses discovered under the pine tree.

The missing four skiers were found fully clothed but having suffered brutal internal injuries. One of the four corpses showed the same signs of blunt force trauma to the head as did Slobodin's. He had apparently been struck by a heavy object. Two of the remaining three corpses had their rib cages crushed inward causing massive internal injury. Stranger still the corpses were not found to have any bruising or soft tissue damage. The doctor in charge of examining the bodies, Dr. Boris Vozrozhdenny was quoted as saying that the damage was beyond a man's capability to cause and was "...equal to that of a car wreck." One of the female team members named Dubanina

was found with her head tilted back and appeared to be
screaming. Her tongue had been removed at its base.

Photo of the "snow man" taken by one of the hikers.

Family members of the victims claimed that the corpses of their loved ones were strangely orange in color and that their hair had lost all the pigmentation. The bodies were also discovered to have higher than normal radiation levels. It is unknown, however, whether this was due to their activities at the Polytechnic Institute or if it was caused by whatever killed them. Campers camping 30 miles to the east of the dead ski team reported seeing strange orange glowing balls of light above the pass during the same time period as it is believed the 'incident' occurred. Because of the bizarre nature of this event and the popularity of the team members involved with the public, Russian investigators were forced to put a lot of effort into solving this mystery. Theories ranged from an attack by 'Wild Men' to and unknown military test of some kind. Wild Men and predators of all kinds were ruled out because no other footprints were discovered except those of the deceased. To this day the official cause of death is a "Compelling unknown source."

In recent years a documentary aired in which the lead investigator for this case for the Russian government admitted that they also found a diary left by one of the women on the expedition. In it she makes a curious statement, "Now we know the snowmen do exist." Along with this revelation came an even bigger one. On one of the cameras used by the expedition an undeveloped role of film showed what appeared to be a Bigfoot like creature in the distance peering out at them from behind a tree. The diary entry and the photograph are damning evidence that this was caused by the Russian version of our Bigfoot, but it does not explain the more paranormal aspects of the wounds on the bodies. Something very, very, scary happened that night to those innocent people and to us paranormal investigators it stands as a signpost to help us remember what our efforts are for.

In the end it is quite simply to identify the phenomenon and ascertain whether the phenomenon is a threat to humans or not. Secondary is whether it confirms our ever-growing scientific understanding of the universe and our reality construct.

Photograph found on camera of the "snowman".

In recent months, the Russian government has reopened the Dyatlov case. We do not know what their findings are currently.

The Guarapiranga Human Mutilation Case is another extremely disturbing paranormal case. This is the case of a corpse discovered outside Sao Paulo, Brazil that had all the same wounds and hallmarks of a classic cattle mutilation.

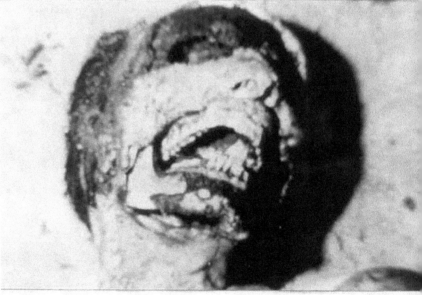

Autopsy photograph of the victim

The victim was apparently discovered near a water reservoir. The official autopsy report has been released by the Legal Medicine Institute, Scientific Police Dept, San Paulo State Public Security Secretary. It details a horrific death. The victim was both alive and paralyzed when these wounds were inflicted. The coroner also believes that these wounds were caused by a machine and that this machine had to be designed specifically for this activity, and not for any other use, because of the precision of the wounds involved. I have spent many a sleepless night contemplating that most horrifying fact.

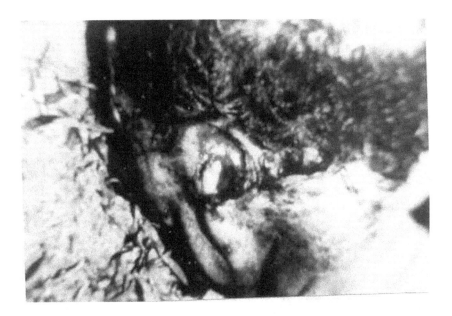

This is an excerpt from the autopsy report:
"EXTERNAL EXAMINATION: We observed: 1) Cut off of the external ear by a slanting incision, with hollowing of soft parts; 2) removal of internal ear with **indications of vital reaction**; 3) enucleation of right and left ocular globes, with signs of blood inside the cavities"
"16) We observed the removal of the right and left orbital areas, emptying of the mouth cavity, pharynx, oropharynx, neck, right

and left armpit area, abdomen, pelvic cavity, right and left groin area".

The body was also completely drained of blood. The use of the term 'Vital reaction' means the person was alive when the wounds were inflicted. This is often denoted by the blue coloring around the wound.

"8) The left and the right armpit areas exhibit a circular discontinuity [round hole], with 4 centimeters of diameter, with regular borders and hollowing of soft parts, with signs of **vital reaction**".

"21) Absence of organs In the pelvis and abdominal cavity due to the removal of all viscera, with signs of tearing and **vital reaction**".

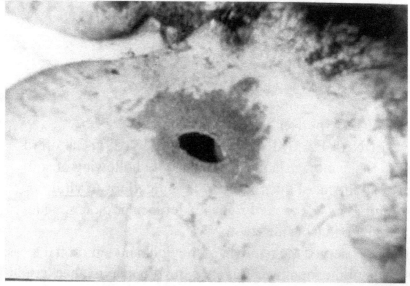

"INTERNAL EXAMINATION: ...after opening the cranial cavity using Griessinger technique we found: 17) unimpaired skullcap; 18) cerebral edema".

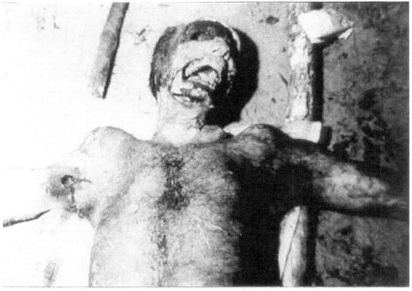

"...acute hemorrhage in multiple traumatisms. There is a component of causa mortis by vague stimulation" [implying cardio-respiratory arrest caused by extreme pain]."The victim shows injuries with vital reaction characteristics, i.e., there is the component "torture". The suggested modus operandi is incisions in soft parts and natural orifices using sucking devices".

"10) Elliptic, elongated incision with 3 cm x 1 cm axis, at the left groin crease."

"14) Removal of the anal orifice with ample incision, oval shaped, elongated, with 15 cm x 8 cm axis"

The rectum was found to be completely cored out the same as in many cattle mutilation cases. The other similarities include the facial wounds, the round puncture wounds and the bloodless bodies. It is also believed that in cattle mutilations the animals are alive as the wounds are inflicted. It is cases like this that spur our efforts forward into discovering and documenting in an undeniable way the existence of predatory paranormal events like these. It has been reported by other researchers that a number of these cases have occurred in the U.S., but this case is the only one we have come across that was supported by an official state autopsy report as well as detailed photographs.

Chapter 4
Murdered by Human Wolves: The Dog Men Of Oklahoma

In the past few months, a very strange case was brought to the P.I.A. for further investigation. This case might just be called the sad case of Katherine Cross, had it not also possessed very ominous undertones of something more paranormal than the reported details of the Katherine Cross tragedy. A few investigators have investigated this mystery but none so much as Mary Franklin, an investigator located in Oklahoma. Mary was kind enough to share her case files spanning a 25-year period of investigation into this mystery. I have begun my own analytical investigation into this case.

In the quiet, sleepy little town of Konawa, Oklahoma. a great mystery unfolded in 1917 and continues to unfold to this day.

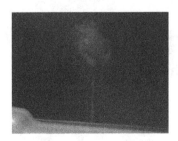

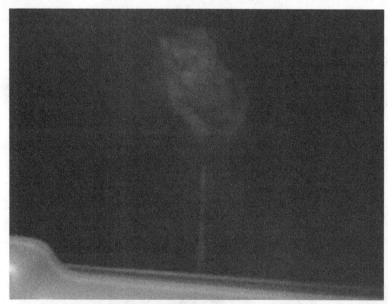

Dogman photo taken in Muskogee, Oklahoma.

The known public facts of this mystery are tragic enough but taken in whole with the substantial amount of other source evidence available, it begins to form a very dark picture. The accepted version of the story is that in October of 1917 a man named Dr. Yates was charged with performing an 'illegal operation' on a woman named Katherine Cross who lived in Konawa along with the Dr. This illegal operation is thought to have been an illegal abortion. The operation caused her death and Dr. Yates was charged with her murder. What is still unexplained about these charges is that they were later lessened to manslaughter before the Dr. was found not guilty of the charges. There is some evidence to suggest that another man in the town of Konawa named Fred O'Neil was instrumental in this outcome and that his father was the judge presiding over the case.

There is scant other information regarding this affair because of the rural nature of the setting of Konawa in 1917. Even today, Konawa only has a resident population of 1400 people. The population in 1917 was less than 100 people. What is known is that shortly after this whole event happened, the Dr. was once again charged with performing an illegal abortion on a woman named Elise Stone. It is known that Fred O'Neil was a teacher at the same school as Elise Stone and it is suspected that he may have been the father of the fatefully aborted child. Just as before, Dr. Yates was acquitted.

Those are the known facts surrounding this headstone. The inscription on the bottom of the headstone remains unexplained currently. 25 years ago, Mary Franklin decided to delve into this case and was met with death threats and a bizarre series of events that clearly indicates something far stranger at hand than the accepted story of Katherine Cross.

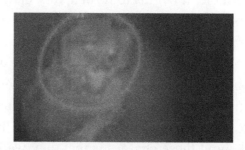

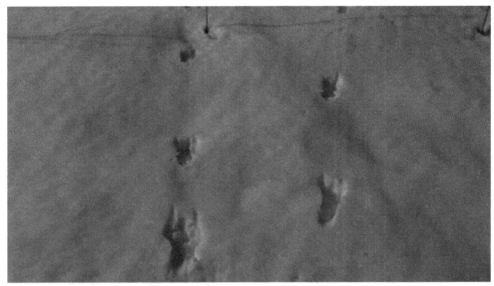

Picture: Double Dog Man tracks in fresh snow discovered by a homesteader named Carol Davies. Notice the three toed print which is the hallmark of the Dog Man. These tracks show two creatures running side by side.

This is where the strangeness increases exponentially in this case. Not long after the discovery of the headstone in Konawa, Oklahoma, other witnesses came forward to report other headstones in small towns in central Oklahoma near Konawa and Ada that also bore the inscription "Murdered by Human Wolves", and some of these headstones were of male victims. One such headstone dating to 1901 still stands in the small, overgrown cemetery of Purcell, Oklahoma. Another headstone bearing the same inscription was also discovered in the small town of Stonewall, Oklahoma. All these towns are in proximity in south central Oklahoma. September 2, 2001 a witness came forward named Michael Greyhawk who lived in yet another small town located near the others named Thackerville. Greyhawk reported that he had been near the lagoon outside of town and witnessed a very strange creature that he described as a "pale looking human male with an elongated face running very quickly on all four's like a dog." He said the creature was able to clear a very tall fence without a sound before disappearing into the woods.

Jack Cary investigating the Lakewood Lycan case with Jc Johnson of Crypto 4 Corners.

photograph of purported Upright walking canine creature taken in rural Oklahoma.

While investigating this case we discovered a cross pattern of information. This presents itself in the form of research done by the preeminent researcher into the Dog Man mystery, Linda Godfrey. In her case files she presents two very interesting encounters that were reported to her. The location of these encounters was south central Oklahoma. These encounters occurred very near the same small towns where headstones have been discovered bearing the inscription "Murdered by Human Wolves."

In 2011, Linda Godfrey was contacted by a school counselor who works near Ada, Oklahoma in south central Oklahoma. She was 5 miles southeast of Ada on a rural back road when she came across a figure walking down the side of the road. As she passed the figure, she was astonished to see a 7-foot-tall upright walking wolf like creature carrying a deer over its right shoulder. She reported that it turned and easily stepped over a fence with its kill and strode off into the woods on its hind legs.

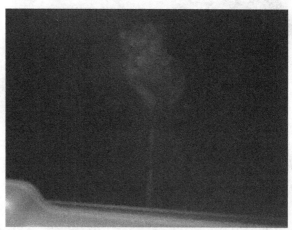

The Onaway photograph, taken by a family out of the back window of their minivan as they fled a Dog Man.

In 1993 two teenagers who were hanging out in their cars on a back road near Okarche, Oklahoma, reported to Linda Godfrey that they too had an encounter with a 7-foot-tall upright walking canine creature that approached their vehicles as they sat chatting. They sped away and report that neither are willing to go into the country anymore, especially at night. These encounters can be found in their entirety in Linda Godfrey's book 'Real Wolfmen, True Encounters in Modern America."

The Dog Man of Lost Creek Wilderness in Colorado is a creature which haunts me. I believe the still frame taken from the original video is probably the best photo we have of a real Dog Man. This creature was unknowingly caught on video while two sasquatch investigators were filming the countryside. A Bigfoot report had come into the group and they dispatched two investigators to go to the scene of the sighting and film what the area looked like. At one point in the video a darker than normal spot can be seen the far distance.

The camera operator tried but was unable to fully focus in at that distance. When the video was slowed down and the frames blown up at 800%, the most terrifying face can clearly be seen peering out from the foliage. The massive forearm of the creature is bent at a 90-degree angle in front of its gigantic pectoral muscles. The arm is also blocking out some of the foliage. If you look closely, then you can see the very iris of the creatures left eye. This was no bear, the creature stood upright for the entire duration and stood approximately 8 ft. tall. The protrusive snout and upright ears can clearly be seen. The creature fits all known eyewitness descriptions of what a Dog Man looks like.

I often lay awake at night thinking about this creature. It is still out there, still roaming around, still watching the people who wander into that area. Lost Creek Wilderness is only a very short distance from my cabin in Colorado. I have spent a considerable amount of time there doing Bigfoot research. Now when I enter the area, I do so with great caution and a fair amount of fear. If an investigator were forced into protecting themselves from such a creature, they might get off a shot............maybe.

What are the Dog Men? I have compiled a list that covers all options available to us as investigators into this phenomenon. The evidence is compelling because it so resembles the evidence for Bigfoot and I KNOW that they exist. In both cases, we have the oral histories of countless indigenous tribes speaking of these creatures. In both cases, we have a large body of very credible people sincerely telling us of their encounters. In both cases, we have physical evidence of the creatures being left. I am quite aware of the bizarre nature of the idea of a half dog, half man creature but I always approach a paranormal investigation the same way. In the words of the great Sir Arthur Conan Doyle, "When you eliminate the impossible, whatever remains, however improbable, has to be the truth."

My list of possibilities came as a byproduct of many years of investigating and analyzing every case I could find.

What are Dogmen? Here is a current list of possible suspected origins:

1. New Species of Canine/Human hybrid through some sort of evolutionary leap not understood by current biological science?

2. Alien creation of some sort sent to perform unknown mission?

3. Etheric manifestation of some sort brought about by ancient Native American worship of humanoid dog headed creatures? (see Xolotle)

4. Inter-dimensional predator?

5. Leftover remains of a 'Soldier Class' of beings from a time when ancient aliens ruled the Earth? (Ancient Alien Theory).

6. These are humans with the genetic ability to 'shape shift' as described in many Native American cultures.

Known Fact: Dr. Melba Ketchum has Dog Man D.N.A. in her possession and the mitochondrial (mother's lineage) is Homo Sapiens in origin. This is also the case in the Bigfoot species. In other words, it appears that whoever fused together the D.N.A. of the creature did the same with the Bigfoot species. They are both the byproduct of the same source whatever that may be.

These are the current possibilities given all known facts and statistics regarding these creatures. In the end, only one of them can be true. How do we begin to eliminate the impossible? The answer to that question is the beginning of solving this mystery.

Jack Cary during field investigation of the Chuska Bigfoot.

Lost Creek Dog Man freeze frame from the video of the creature

This creature stood upright for a very long time. Notice the forearm of the creature bent at a right angle, blocking both the foliage and his left pectoral muscle. An upright ear can also be seen on the left side of the head. Because of the distance of the footage from the subject, the image had to be magnified 800% in order to see the creature.

In this frame the creature moved slightly, then tilted its head up and sniffed the air as though it could smell the presence of humans.

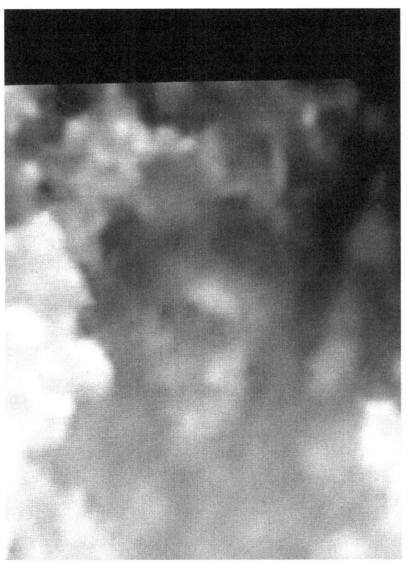

Extreme close up causes pixilation, but the iris of the right eye becomes visible.

Tracking the Lakewood Lycan - Unknown Cryptid Predator Roaming Suburbs of Denver

On March 23, 2014 a witness emerged who claimed to have an encounter with an unknown canine like cryptid animal in his friend's yard in an affluent neighborhood in the Denver suburbs. This encounter took place at approximately 2:00 a.m. as the witness was walking his friend's dog.

The details of the encounter firmly place this sighting into the growing column of 'Dog Man' sightings now taking place. We have been able to determine through our ongoing investigation that this neighborhood backs up to a completely undeveloped wilderness area that eventually turns into a State park, and then into the open wilderness of the front mountain range of Denver.

According to witness testimony, the neighborhood suffers from a coyote problem and he and his friend had previously discovered evidence of rabbit kills in the backyard of the property. This property is a large lot in an affluent neighborhood stretching 1.5 acres. In the early morning hours of March 14th, the witness took his friend's dog out to the backyard. The dog was always accompanied outside because of the ongoing coyote problem. While in the backyard with the aging pug dog the witness had an encounter with an upright walking canine creature. The eyewitness account is as follows. The Phantoms and Monsters news site first broke this story and I and my late great mentor J.C. Johnson were investigating this case on their behalf.

"I was standing around 20 yards from the back door and around 10 yards from the iron fence. I had my back to the iron fence and the dogs close. This is where I feel like I sound weird but here goes. I heard what to me sounded like hoof beats running extremely fast up from behind me. In my head I had just enough time to think why am I hearing hooves??? I knew a horse made no sense, but I know the sound of hooves. I knew an animal was coming straight at me. I turned expecting a coyote even though the sound made no sense. As I turned around to the fence, something I can hardly describe had just launched off the ground from the driveway. It was moving extremely fast and cleared the fence easily. I was more like it had jumped from farther back in the driveway so it's trajectory would land it closer to us at that speed. As i said, we were only 10 yards from the fence, but this thing was just moving so fast.

I would guess I had about 1 second tops to register the sound I heard (thanks to the concrete on the driveway) and realize something was happening. Since I expected a coyote as I turned around all I could think of was to stick out my arms and make myself look bigger as well as kind of shield the dogs near me. I screamed "NO" as loud as I could an caught this thing in the flashlight beam as I turned around. It was coming straight at me and I had a split second to step aside slightly as it landed just a few feet from me. It was still going full speed when it hit the ground. Like fast predator speed. It touched down quickly on all fours but immediately rose back up to two legs and continued running at full speed toward the back fence. My dog gave a very short chase (just a few steps really) but could never keep up at that speed. This thing continued running straight at the back, stone fence very fast. The back fence is around 30 yards from where I was standing when this took place and 8 ft tall. I heard its steps moving away and followed it with the flashlight. I did not actually see it jump the back fence, but I lost it in the confusion heading that direction almost too quickly to have stopped. Also, I didn't hear any steps through the wide gravel border surrounding the fence. I can only assume it cleared the back fence as easily as it cleared the front even though it is much higher."

Jc Johnson and I identified the pathway by which the creature was able to gain access to this neighborhood. This identification has also led us to an area where we believe the creature and/or creatures are sleeping during the day. This area would allow almost completely undisturbed cover and is well within travelling range of the 'Lakewood Lycan' encounter. The following is the eyewitness sketch of the creature he encountered that night. This sketch as well as the witness's observations, match perfectly with the details reported by many other 'Dog Man' witnesses.

- Never saw hands or feet well but it sounded like talons on the concrete
- Not wings but extra skin with a cloak like look
- Skin is Matte black and leathery looking very short hair
- Not a hunch back really, it was running very fast towards me and bent forward
- Eyes are yellow, larger than they appear here as it passed me - slightly hooded by the brow + shadows
- larger canine teeth visible as it passed

Chapter 5
The Club of Rome, Eisenhower's Great Granddaughter, and the Breakaway Civilization.

Researchers around the world have come across a line of evidence in support of the theory that there is a secret Mars colony already established and operating. This line of evidence starts with the Club of Rome. The Club of Rome is a global think-tank and its members include such notary's as Henry Kissinger. Founded in 1968, the Club of Rome was commissioned by MIT scientists to study global overpopulation. Their findings were published in a book titled 'The Limits to Growth' in 1972. What they determined was shocking in the extreme and according to them the earth would run out of natural resources in as little as 100 years. It was concluded by them that there were only three courses of action that could be undertaken to combat the problem. The first was to implement policies world-wide to slow the overall birth rate. The world's seventh billion person was born this year so we can see how that turned out. The second course of action was to implement policies to speed up the death rate of the world's existing population. This has spawned any number of interesting conspiracy theories regarding world depopulation and manipulation of the world's food supply. The third course of action was given the name Alternative 3 and has to do with the colonization of space.

At some point in their studies they became convinced that alternative 1 and alternative 2 would be near to impossible to achieve. It was therefore concluded by these very powerful people that colonization of space was the only way to ensure survival of the human species once the world descended into all-out war over the precious few resources left.

In recent years, a very outspoken and interesting witness came forward with a personal statement on her website as well as granting a radio interview. This witness was none other than Laura Magdalene Eisenhower the great granddaughter of President Eisenhower. She claims to have been approached by intelligence agents about joining a secret Mars colony project. Ms. Eisenhower disclosed her attempted secret recruitment and manipulation into the project by trained intelligence agents between April 2006 and January 2007. Ki Lia, a Stanford educated artist, futurist and colleague of Ms. Eisenhower has provided corroborating firsthand account of both her and Laura Eisenhower's attempted recruitment into the project. This information is available on her website.

We have long reported that the world's most experienced Remote Viewers, many of them with C.I.A. or military intelligence backgrounds have targeted what appears to be structures and people on Mars. These Remote Viewers are part of the farsight.org group led by Dr. Courtney Brown. The following is a video of their findings presented by Dr. Brown himself.

A famous U.F.O researcher and author named Richard Dolan has coined the term 'Breakaway Civilization' to describe this project. He asks a most interesting question' "Could a group of people with unlimited funding and apparent access to alien technology constitute a Breakaway civilization." One that was paid for by American tax payer dollars? The evidence is mounting that these structures do exist and that a fantastic secret has been kept from the world.

In recent years Dr. Courtney Brown's organization, known as the Farsight Institute, released the results of a very compelling experiment that they undertook utilizing the most proficient military grade remote viewers on the planet. The experiment was based on a photograph obtained from N.A.S.A. J.P.L. Lab and that is available to the public at large online. This experiment used nine remote viewers with over ten years each of operational experience and with impressive track records. 24 sessions were conducted on the target in the photograph. The photograph is clearly of a dome like structure located on the surface of Mars. The amazing thing about this photograph is that it clearly shows liquid being ejected from a massive pipe like structure which protrudes from the dome. All sessions conducted were both "solo" and "blind", meaning that the Remote Viewers were both completely alone and had no prior knowledge of the target they had been assigned to remote view.

The following link is to the original source of the photo which was captured for N.A.S.A. by Milan Space Science Systems:

http://www.msss.com/moc_gallery/m07_m12/images/M11/M1100099.html

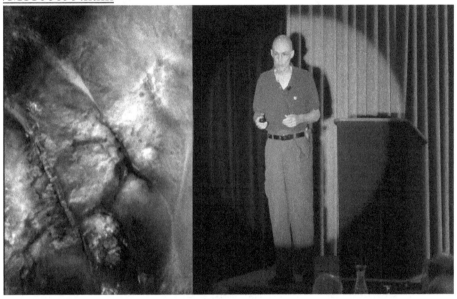

The results of the experiment were breathtaking and a large amount of information about this structure was gained by the viewers. The results concluded that the domes in the photographs are artificial. There are current inhabitants in the domes. The original builders of the domes are ancient. The current inhabitants do not fully understand the technology, and the inhabitants are missing spare parts. These domes have enormous power generating technology. Almost every viewer reported intense light flashing from the domes. They also were able to ascertain that there is a sense of despondency among the current inhabitants. The current inhabitants accepted this assignment as a hardship assignment and knew that they could never return home once they had accepted it. The experiment went on to conclude that there was no extraterrestrial content to the RV data, meaning that these were human subjects. Lynn Buchanan, one of the most proficient remote viewers in the group picked up on elements of this being a "black" military operation.

This is interesting considering the newly discovered TR-3B patent. Those who have argued against the existence of a secret Mars colony have largely done so based on the idea that we did not possess a spacecraft with the technological capability to get people and supplies efficiently to the surface of Mars. The patent and surrounding evidence for the TR-3B clearly makes that argument untenable. The testimony of British hacker Gary Mckinnon even ties in perfectly with what appears to be a large and growing body of evidence that the greatest military "black" operation has been executed with precision and what appears to be a large amount of success. I believe that the Mars colony may even have ties to the missing 2.3 trillion dollars reported by the pentagon. Clif High's web bot has also detected a large amount of data concerning a secret space program and his reports indicate that this program will be revealed to the public in the next few years.

Recently there has been much attention being given by various researchers into a patent that was filed in 2004, that describes in detail the super-secret U.S. Airforce craft known as the TR-3B Astra. Although this patent was filed in 2004, it has only been discovered recently by those investigating U.F.O. activity. The discovery of this patent is important because it has long been suspected by U.F.O. researchers that the many triangular U.F.O. sightings happening around the world were, in fact, a super-secret man-made craft that were a part of the Aurora program. The development of this craft was funded by the National Reconnaissance Office, the N.S.A. and the C.I.A. The inventor's name is listed as John St. Clair. This name immediately set off alarm bells with the P.I.A. because anyone who has investigated ancient mysteries will be well acquainted with the name St. Clair. This is a royal bloodline in Scotland that helped to provide both safe harbor to the last remnants of the Templar Knights, as well as being instrumental in the evolution of the Templar Knights into the Freemasonic brotherhood.

The craft in the patent is described as:

"A spacecraft with a triangular hull and vertical electrostatic line charges on each corner that produce a horizontal electric field parallel to the sides of the hull. This field, interacting with a plane wave emitted by antennas on the side of the hull, generates a force per volume combining both lift and propulsion."

Recently video of this craft was leaked to LiveLeak.com, the following link shows this craft in action. https://www.liveleak.com/view?i=08b_1362520923

The patent goes onto state that the craft uses an electrostatic propulsion system augmented by magnetic vortex generators. This in effect allows for a slight space time curvature. It is estimated that the development of this craft ran into the many billions of dollars but that much of the technology for its development was available to elements of the military industrial complex as early as the mid 1980's. The craft is covered with a stealth polymer skin that allows it to play havoc with existing radar detection systems. The discovery of this patent as well as the many videos now depicting these craft is absolute confirmation that, not only do these craft exist but that they can account for the long running mystery of both the Belgium U.F.O. wave and the Illinois Triangle U.F.O. sightings.

The Belgium U.F.O. wave lasted from November 29, 1989 until April of 1990. This wave included hundreds of eyewitness accounts including accounts by police officers. Every eyewitness account describes exactly the craft described in the patent recently discovered.

U.F.O photograph taken during the famous Belgian U.F.O. flap.

On January 5, 2000 a triangular craft which matches the description of the TR-3B was spotted over the skies of Illinois. This craft was tracked by officers on the ground who were able to remain in radio contact with each other during the event. Their testimonies have appeared in documentaries on the subject. One of the principle witnesses was officer Ed Barton who provided an eyewitness sketch.

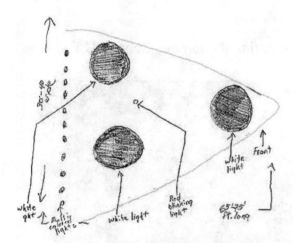

Eyewitness sketch by Officer Ed Barton.

Notice the obvious similarity between Officer Barton's sketch and sketches drawn by eyewitnesses to the Belgium U.F.O. wave

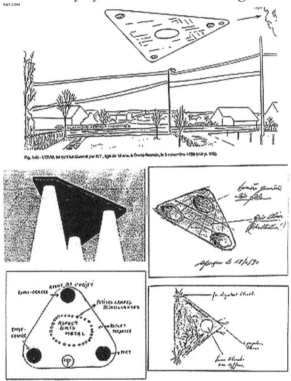

Eyewitness sketches of the triangular U.F.O. seen during the Belgium U.F.O. wave.

Researchers now have a basis for the belief in a secret space program. The P.I.A. is certain that this program exists and that it ties in directly to the secret Mars colony that was discovered by Dr. Courtney Brown and the Farsight.org institute.

This amazing remote viewing experiment shows clearly that the colony exists and even discovered information on its inhabitants. We also discuss the testimony of Dwight D. Eisenhower's great granddaughter, Laura Magdalene Eisenhower. She claims to have been approached to take part in this secret Mars colony. Was the Club of Rome the impetus for the program to be started? If the Martian colony is real and it sure looks to be, then it tells us a great deal. It tells us that those involved were powerful enough, wealthy enough, entrenched in the black budget operations enough, to pull off the greatest event in human history, right under the noses of the world's ever growing population.

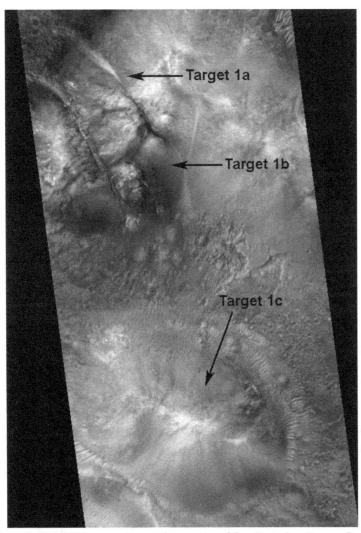

Picture of the Mars colony discovered by Dr. Courtney Brown and the Farsight.org remote viewers.

The War in Heaven, The Death of Mars, And the Reptilians Among Us

Recently the organization of world class remote viewers headed by Dr. Courtney Brown blindly targeted a very well-known verse in the bible, Revelations 12:7. This verse was chosen as a target because of its seemingly omnipresence among all the world's ancient oral and written histories. The outcome of the targeting was as surprising as it was unexpected. The verse Revelations 12:7 states:

"Then a war broke out in heaven: Michael and his angels fought against the dragon, and the dragon and his angels fought back. But the dragon was not strong enough, and no longer was any place found in heaven for him and his angels."

The results of the remote viewing sessions which stretched over a long period of time concluded that at one point the planet Mars was inhabited by a humanoid species not dissimilar to modern humans here on Earth. This civilization was attacked by an aggressor species which were reptilian in nature and who invaded Mars to take control of its resources. The reptilian species origin was a planet that today is identified as Malbec or Tiamat among ancient cultures. The humanoid species on Mars resisted the invasion and this led to a devastating war between the two planets. The reptilians apparently launched several nuclear based weapons targeting Mars. This provides an explanation for why scientists like Dr. John Brandenburg have lectured publicly about there being massive nuclear explosions on the surface of Mars at some point in the ancient past. The remote viewers determined that the Martian race was losing the war badly and made on last attempt at saving themselves. They developed and deployed a weapon of such destructive power that when it hit the planet Tiamat where the reptilians resided, it literally blew up the entire planet and this resulted in what is today known as the asteroid belt. This also provides an explanation for why only half the surface of Mars is covered in meteoric craters while the other half remains untouched. These craters were the results of the debris left over from Tiamat colliding on the surface of Mars.

The remnants of the reptilian species who were largely in orbit around Mars at the time of the destruction of their home planet, were left with only one option and that was to travel to Earth in order to find a place of survival. The Martian species also launched space craft which were like giant Arks that set off for the nearest habitable planet, Earth. This is where many cross currents begin to coincide with one another. Many U.F.O. researchers and readers have accumulated a mountain of evidence about this reptilian species.

The farsight.org group targeted Area 51 and discovered that, in fact, there is an enormous underground facility housing many of these creatures and that they are apparently working in cooperation with the U.S. military industrial complex. This cooperation seems to include the trading of exotic weaponized technology in exchange for allowing them to reside on this planet. What other agreements have been reached are merely speculation at this point. The base at Dulce, New Mexico is yet another example of this arrangement and whistle blowers like Phil Schneider have spoken openly about their personal experiences dealing with these creatures while working as contractors for the U.S. Military.

This also leads us into the amazing amount of material that has been coming out about the possibility of Antarctica having vast ancient alien ruins which are now being excavated by the U.S. military. Several whistleblowers have recently come forth to the famous researcher and award-winning journalist Linda Moultan Howe to discuss what they have seen in Antarctica. In short, it appears that the humanoids which travelled here from a decimated Mars civilization landed on what is now Antarctica at some point in the ancient past when it was far more habitable.

These insiders claim that not only have strange bodies been found but that also a new form of technology that might just revolutionize how the earth's population generates power. Clif High at the Web Bot has also been quite adamant that according to his ALTA reports there is a ton of language coming out about Antarctica and that in the very near future information will be leaked that will awaken the public to what has been found there. It can be stated then that 'The War In Heaven', as described by the remote viewers at Farsight.org, has brought together many pieces of a puzzle that is now beginning to present us with a breathtaking picture.

The former lead singer of the Smashing Pumpkins stated in an interview on the Howard Stern show that he witnessed a person he knew who literally 'shifted' into something non-human. The announcement shocked both Stern and the listening public. Corgan was asked about his appearance on the Alex Jones show and that's when Corgan revealed his own paranormal experience,

"Not to add to the conspiracy, but I've had paranormal experiences in my life that sort of lend itself into that category," he said. Corgan appeared embarrassed to speak of his experiences and did not provide many details but stated that he once saw a person he knew personally transform into something he "cannot explain".

"Let's just say I was with somebody once and I saw a transformation I can't explain," said Corgan.

"The person transformed into something other than human?" Stern asked.

"Yes, I saw it." Corgan replied.

Robin Quivers the show's co-host then asked if he was on drugs at the time and he replied, "I was totally sober."

He went on to state that the person later acknowledged the transformation but would not explain to him how it happened.

"I'm being vague on purpose," Corgan said.

Many people have come forward to claim publicly that they have witnessed the same thing and that often the transformation seems to be into a 'reptilian' alien. Many famous researchers have published accounts of vast conspiracy taking place on this planet dealing with these reptilian entities. The researcher and author David Icke is chief among the growing number of people making this claim. Is this what Corgan saw? Hopefully, he will give more details in time. Bigelow told Lara Logan of 60 minutes that he became interested in U.F.O.'s after his grandparents had a close encounter on a canyon road right outside of Las Vegas.

In recent years Robert Bigelow founded the N.I.D.S. or National Institute of Discovery Science. This group was originally formed to study the odd events then happening at the now famous 'Skinwalker Ranch'. He assembled a team of world class scientists to study a wide array of paranormal activity taking place on this remote Utah ranch. The full chronicle of their mind-bending experiences on this remote ranch was published in the book 'Hunt for the Skinwalker', written by journalist George Knapp and scientist Cohlm Kelleher who was a member of the team. Robert Bigelow's group works in close concert with the U.S. government concerning U.F.O.'s and Aliens. His discussion with Logan was startling. The CBS 60 Minutes transcript of their conversation is:

Lara Logan: Do you believe in aliens?

Robert Bigelow: I'm absolutely convinced. That's all there is to it.

Lara Logan: Do you also believe that UFOs have come to Earth?

Robert Bigelow: There has been and is an existing presence, an ET presence. And I spent millions and millions and millions -- I probably spent more as an individual than anybody else in the United States has ever spent on this subject.

Lara Logan: Is it risky for you to say in public that you believe in UFOs and aliens?

Robert Bigelow: I don't give a damn. I don't care.

Lara Logan: You don't worry that some people will say, "Did you hear that guy, he sounds like he's crazy"?

Robert Bigelow: I don't care.

Lara Logan: Why not?

Robert Bigelow: It's not going to make a difference. It's not going to change reality of what I know.

Lara Logan: Do you imagine that in our space travels we will encounter other forms of intelligent life?

Robert Bigelow: You don't have to go anywhere.

Lara Logan: You can find it here? Where exactly?

Robert Bigelow: It's just like right under people's noses.

The FAA confirmed to 60 Minutes that for years, they referred all U.F.O. sightings to a company owned by Robert Bigelow. The recently declassified Pentagon U.F.O. Program also studied other paranormal activity that related to the U.F.O. program. The newest document to emerge from George Knapp's I-team investigation at KLAS T.V. in Las Vegas, state's that these various phenomena seemed to fall under a "Panoply". This means simply that along with the craft they were monitoring there were other types of activity also taking place.

"The phenomenon also involved a whole panoply of bizarre activity that included bizarre creatures, poltergeist activity, invisible entities, orbs of light, animal and human injuries and much more."

This is interesting because Robert Bigelow has been shown to be connected to the secret Pentagon U.F.O. program and is well known among researchers into the paranormal because of his role in various U.F.O. and paranormal investigations on behalf of the U.S. government. George Knapp chronicled Brigalow's role in the now famous Skinwalker Ranch investigation in his book 'Hunt for the Skinwalker'. He detailed Bigelow's investigation into the happenings there through his organization the N.I.D.S. or National Institute for Discovery Science. What the team encountered there is the very definition of paranormal and included all the above mentioned, bizarre creatures, poltergeist, invisible entities, orbs of light, animal and human injuries etc. The N.I.D.S.'s investigation revealed that there was interdimensional activity occurring at Skinwalker Ranch.

Now a new document from the Pentagon reveals that all the same activity Bigelow's group experienced then also seemed to be interconnected with the U.F.O. phenomenon they were studying. Could this be telling us that some U.F.O.'s might be originating in another dimension?

The Report goes onto state something very scary:

"The evidence was multiplying that the UFO phenomenon was capable of manipulating and distorting human perception and

therefore eyewitness testimony of UFO activity was becoming increasingly untrustworthy."

And then it details a new way of investigating U.F.O effects on human beings and that this new technique was a revolution in assessing the threat level of U.F.O,'s. We find this to be the most disturbing statement of all:

"The BAASS approach was to view the human body as a readout system for UFO effects by utilizing forensic technology, the tools of immunology, cell biology, genomics and neuroanatomy for in depth study of the effects of UFOs on humans. This approach marked a dramatic shift away from the traditional norms of relying on eyewitness testimony as the central evidentiary arm in UFO investigations. The approach aimed to bypass UFO deception and manipulation of human perception by utilizing molecular forensics to decipher the biological consequences of the phenomenon."

The result of applying this new approach was a revolution in delineating the threat level of UFOs. This is a very important document because it clearly states that the intelligence behind the U.F.O. phenomenon is utilizing deception and manipulation for the purpose of achieving some end. We can speculate as to what their agenda may be, but It is our estimation that work of Dr. David M. Jacobs points clearly to a type of 'soft invasion'. His newest work 'They Walk Among Us' is compelling in its claims that alien-human hybrids are now being deployed into our society and appear completely human but with one little nasty difference. They can manipulate the thoughts and actions of those around them. One can only surmise that the government must be aware of such activity and as such, will act accordingly.

Rendlesham U.F.O. Event and The Mystery Of Hy Brasil In The Binary Code Received By Jim Penniston

The Rendlesham U.F.O. incident is world famous, having been the subject of several U.F.O documentary and other television specials. This event occurred shortly after midnight on December 26, 1980 at the joint U.S. and British air base located in the U.K. During this incident a triangular craft approximately 9 feet long and 4 to 5 feet high landed near the base. The craft was glowing with orange, blue, and yellow lights. Jim Penniston was able to approach the craft and touch it. When he touched the craft, he claims it somehow telepathically downloaded a 16 page binary code into his mind. This code stuck in his mind and he wrote it down the day after the incident. This code was not translated till decades later and to the amazement of the computer scientist who translated the code, it contained a mysterious message.

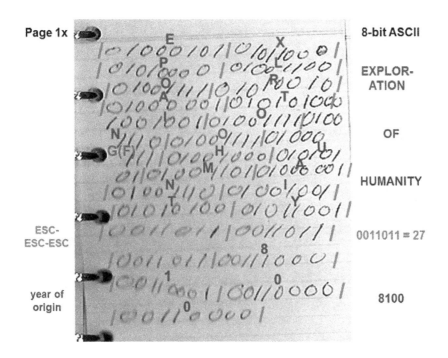

The translation of the code contains a message indicating that this craft was somehow monitoring the "continuous advance of humanity." It then goes on to list several locations around the world which today are considered quite mysterious and somehow linked to events of the past on this planet which are lost to us.

EXPLORATION OF HUMANITY 666 8100

52.0942532N 13.131269W (Hy Brasil)

CONTINUOUS FOR PLANETARY ADVAN???

An independent translation of the Woodbridge binary code by Jim Penniston is very similar, except for the assigned origin

FOURTH COODINATE CONTINUOT UQS CbPR BEFORE

26.763177N 89.117768W (Caracol, Belize)

34.800272N 111.843567W (Sedona, Arizona)

29.977836N 31.131649E (Great Pyramid in Giza, Egypt)

14.701505S 75.167043W (Nazca Lines in Peru)

36.256845N 117.100632E (Tai Shan Qu, China)

37.110195N 25.372281E (Portal at Temple of Apollo in Naxos, Greece)

EYES OF YOUR EYES

ORIGIN 52.0942532N 13.131269W (Hy Brasil)

ORIGIN YEAR 8100

The message contains the location for an island known to ancient cartographers as Hy Brasil. The name comes from the Celtic word Braseal which referred to the Celtic King of the World. What is fascinating about the inclusion of Hy Brasil is that it doesn't exist. All of the other sites listed exist on planet Earth but not Hy Brasil. In history there are quite a few ancient maps which depict the mythical island. It was always depicted off the western coast of Ireland and as being perfectly round with a single river running like a band across it from east to west. To add to the confusion, explorers like the Scottish sea captain John Nisbet reported to have found the island on his voyage from France to Ireland. A follow up expedition undertaken by the sea captain Alexander Johnson confirmed the existence of the island. The last reported sighting of the island was made in 1872 by Robert O'Flaherty and T.J. Westropp. Westropp claimed to have visited the island on three previous occasions and was so captivated by it that he brought his whole family to see it on his last expedition. There they claimed to have seen the island appear out of nowhere only to disappear again.

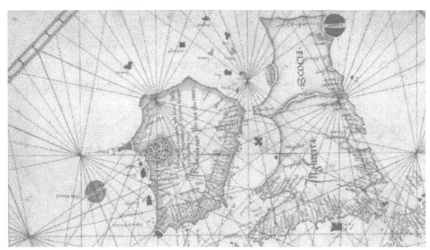

The Nautical chart of Western Europe (1473) shows Hy-Brasil in a circular shape (British Library)

The Rendlesham Forest U.F.O. incident is considered by most investigators to be one of the most highly credible U.F.O. incidents to ever be chronicled. This incident had numerous military witnesses who even after decades of time have remained adamant about their collective experience on that fateful night.

The real mystery to me, is why the message contained the geographical location for an island that appears not to exist and whose historical references are all shrouded in mystical lore and mystery.

The Rendlesham Forest incident seems to back up my new theory. This probe craft appears to have originated from this Type 3 civilization and was assigned the task of monitoring our "continuous planetary advance". The inclusion of the coordinates for Hy Brasil is a very telling clue in this mystery. Only one of two possibilities could be the case. Either the Type 3 civilization from which the probe originated was programmed with an error or the island must exist. Any and all modern day attempts to prove that the island was now a submerged land mass have failed and there quite simply is no evidence of a land mass off the coast of Ireland that would ever have passed as an island.

If the probe was programmed with an error, then we have discovered that the Type 3 civilization is not perfect, and they do make errors. If the probe was not programmed with an error, then what was Hy Brasil?

Chapter 6

Is There A 'Hobbit' Species Living in Minnesota?

Every day the P.I.A. and Crypto 4 Corners comes across something which seems to stretch the boundaries of our known reality. As always, we endeavor to filter through the 'white noise' inherent in paranormal investigations. This comes in the form obvious hoaxes and other misinformation that occurs on a regular basis. In our quest to discover the real evidence of the paranormal happenings and beings among us, we have often come across jaw dropping evidence that a multi array of threatening paranormal happenings are, in fact, taking place.

Recently the founder of Crypto 4 Corners, Jc Johnson, began to investigate sightings and Native American lore describing a species of Hominin like the recent discovery of Homo Floresiensis on the island of Flores off the coast of Indonesia. The remains of this species were discovered in the Liang Bua cave on the remote Indonesian island of Flores.

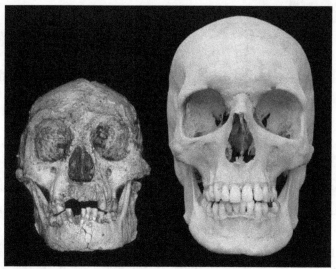
'Hobbit' Skull next to the skull of homo sapiens.

The difference in our on-going investigation is that the species being reported to us, is in Minnesota and not some far off island. In the discovery of the Homo Floresiensis species, which has now been determined by leading experts as being a non-human species, is a scientific precedent for the following photographic evidence that was recently collected in the field by Jc Johnson. Could it be that the Ojibwa Indian lore of the 'Little People of Minnesota' is based entirely in fact and remains a major mystery to be solved? One compelling pattern which emerges is the similarity between the discovery of Homo Floresiensis and descriptions in the Hockomoc swamp in the Bridgewater Triangle of the Puckwudgie creature and descriptions of the Bagwajiwininni or Hobbit of Minnesota. The Puckwudgie is almost identical in description to Ojibwa Indian descriptions of the 'Bagwajiwinini' or Hobbits of Northern

Minnesota. There have been modern day encounters with the Puckwudgie from credible witnesses (See William Russo's account). In the darker parts of the Lore surrounding the Hobbits of Minnesota we find hints and implications of human abduction and in this way could be connected in some way with the over-all alien abduction phenomenon. One modern
day disappearance attributed to the 'Bagwajiwinini' is the strange case of Kory Kelley in 2007 in Minnesota. This case was also included in the cases of David Paulides and the Missing 411 project

Museum recreation of the 'Hobbit' species discovered in Indonesia.

The Hobbits of Flores were not a particularly advanced species. They were only making the most rudimentary of tools and the on-going work on the island has shown that the species was openly hunting several species on the island including a species of now extinct pygmy elephant and a 6 ft. tall Ostrich like bird. Charred remains of the hunts were discovered showing that this species had harnessed the ability to create fire.

X-ray of one of the 'Hobbits' discovered in Indonesia.

These Minnesota creatures are said to roam freely in the darkened under growth of the dense Bracken Ferns of the area and to make their homes underground. There are, of course, many tales around the world of such Little People, not least among these are the Irish stories of Leprechauns. In some Southwest Native American stories, it is said that these creatures cherish salt among all else and will gladly trade gold for it.

Some researchers into this area have even linked the so called 'Lost Dutchman's Mine' with these Hobbits. One source known to the P.I.A. claims the gold attributed to the Lost Dutchman's Mine was obtained through trade with this species.

Recently while in the field, investigating recent sighting of these Hobbits of Minnesota, Jc Johnson, founder of Crypto 4 Corners International, was able to obtain the following photographic evidence for the existence of the 'Hobbits of Minnesota."

Judy Cline gets credit for finding the
humanoid peeking from the ferns.
Ron Shaw is on the left.

Our investigation is ongoing as we utilize the latest in technology and intelligence techniques in order to gain an advantage over this and other types of possibly threatening paranormal activity. We will keep the public updated as we continue to make strides into understanding this most improbable and perplexing mystery.

Chapter 7

The Abduction of Bigfoot? The Link Between Sasquatch and E.T.'s

The link between E.T.'s and the species we refer to as Bigfoot or Sasquatch is very nebulous at this time. A body of evidence, however, does exist clearly showing that not only is there a clear connection but that this connection appears to be a strong connection and the interaction appears to be ongoing. There is a pattern of interaction between E.T.'s and Sasquatch which has been witnessed by many civilian witnesses as well as being witnessed by seasoned, professional, investigators. Historical examples of some of these cases are as follows:

In August of 2008, Brad Steiger, the renowned author and investigator of U.F.O.'s reported receiving a journal from a man who claimed that it was his grandfather's and dated back to 1888. The journal held many entries describing a very interesting encounter this man's grandfather had while in Humboldt county California in 1888. Steiger reported that this journal came from James C. Wyatt of Memphis, Tennessee and that it appeared to be completely authentic. In the journal the elder Wyatt discussed how he had to winter with a local tribe in the "Big Woods country" of the Humboldt line and that while there he witnessed a man carrying large quantities of raw meet to a nearby cave. When queried as to why he was doing this the man bade Wyatt to follow him. Wyatt followed the man into the cave and discovered that a very large, hairy, man-like creature was inside sitting cross-legged. The creature was covered in long, shiny, black hair and appeared to have no neck. The head was described as sitting directly on the shoulders. In 2008, Steiger wrote:

" Wyatt visited the man-beast in the cave more than a dozen times. After much questioning, and receiving two pounds of tobacco, a compass, and an axe, one of the men from the tribe took Wyatt to a high pinnacle of rock one clear night to tell him of the creature's origin.

"Crazy Bear," as the thing was called by the Indians, had been brought to the "Big Woods" from the stars. A "small moon" had flown down like a swooping eagle and had landed on a plateau a few miles away from the tribe's encampment. The beast in the cave and two other "crazy bears" had been flung out of the "moon" before the craft had once again soared off to the stars.

The man told Wyatt that other "crazy bears" had been left in the vicinity over the years. Wyatt's guide and several of his fellow villagers had occasionally seen the "men" who put the crazy bears off the small moons. They did, nor look like the giant hairy ones, but appeared to be more like men such as themselves. The men from the small moon had much shorter hair than the tribe's people, though, and they wore shiny clothing. They always waved to the Indians in a friendly manner before they closed the door in their small moon and flew back to the stars.

The crazy bears had been led to the village by the Indians, and at no time had the hairy giants offered any resistance to their benefactors. The Indians believed that the crazy bears from the stars had been sent to bring them powerful medicine, and they would not permit the creatures to stray away lest they be captured by rival tribes. "

Other historical sightings of note include:

1973 Mrs. Raefa Heitfield of Cincinnati, Ohio reported waking at 2:30 a.m. to get a glass of water and noticed outside of her window in an adjacent parking lot, a cone of light about 7 feet in diameter shining down from the sky. Nearby she saw movement and noticed a large, grayish Bigfoot move out of the darkness into the cone of light. Moments later the creature and the cone of light vanished.

A few days later, on October 25th, 1973 in Fayette county, Pennsylvania; a group of farmers reported seeing a large dome shaped U.F.O. which was brightly lit and approximately 100 feet in diameter. As the farmers drove nearer the U.F.O. they caught sight of two large Sasquatch creatures. The farmer's son is reputed to have taken a shot with his rifle at one of the creatures. It was at this time the U.F.O. disappeared and the creatures escaped into the deep woods never to be seen again.

In the past few years the Crypto 4 Corners team headed up by J.C. Johnson, discovered a so-called track line of Sasquatch prints on extremely remote Navajo Reservation land. What was interesting about this track line of 18-inch-long, 6-inch-wide, footprints is that the prints just suddenly stop in the middle of a field where the topography doesn't change and where the prints should have continued. It is as if the creature leaving the prints simply disappeared into thin air. What was even more peculiar is that the prints began as a walking stride of 5 feet and then suddenly elongated to a 7 ft. stride. This indicated to us that this creature suddenly started running shortly before its track line of prints stopped. What was this creature running from? In such a remote area, a creature of that size and stature would have little to run from unless the threat was one from above?

19-inch footprint discovered in remote northern New Mexico.
This print was one of dozens that led across an entire field.

My mentor Jc Johnson, founder of Crypto 4 Corners.

The Alien abduction phenomenon which has been meticulously documented by such academics as Dr. David M. Jacobs and the late Dr. John E. Mack has one pattern which is reoccurring time and again and that is the collection of D.N.A. by the alien entities perpetrating the abductions. It is the working theory of the P.I.A. that likely, members of the Sasquatch species are also being abducted for their D.N.A. It could well be that they are being abducted simply because they possess some human D.N.A. The fact that they possess some human D.N.A. and the fact that humans are being abducted for the collection and use of their D.N.A. is a link far too strong to dismiss and indicates that these creatures are in all probability a part of the same genetic testing and experimentation that members of the human species are now enduring.

In at least 20 percent of all credible U.F.O. sightings, a Bigfoot is also spotted in close proximity. This is a pattern first noticed by the late great John Keel, author of The Mothman Prophecies.

Sasquatch: The Current State of Affairs.

Many people interested in Cryptozoology are quite unaware of the current state of affairs, as it relates to the full discovery of the Sasquatch species and the resulting acceptance by the public at large. In the course of this previous Summer, Crypto 4 Corners, which is the cryptozoological wing of the P.I.A., made huge strides in proving once and for all the existence of Sasquatch. In the course of a two-day period C4C was able to document multiple footprints left at two separate D.N.A. deposit sites separated by approximately 80 miles of terrain. The collection of these D.N.A. deposits, one of which also had an eyewitness to the D.N.A. being left, were supervised by the Executive Director of the University of New Mexico,

Gallup. These samples were then sealed and shared with Dr. Jeff Meldrum at Idaho State University as part of a new Sasquatch Genome Study. The results are likely to shock not only the established community of Sasquatch researchers but the public as well. Recently, Dr. Meldrum discussed this new endeavor on Coast to Coast A.M. radio with George Noory.

Both genome studies corroborated one another but they were interpreted in completely different ways. In both genome studies the mitochondrial D.N.A. or the mother's lineage proved to be homo sapiens! The first genome had over 300 samples sent from researchers all over North America and this was present in many of the samples. The remainder of the samples were shown to be known animals. The second genome was interpreted as the samples being contaminated with human D.N.A. by the testing geneticist. But those samples too possessed mitochondrial D.N.A. from homo sapiens.

The other D.N.A. from the father's lineage was what perplexed both studies and again it was interpreted in two different ways. In the first genome the geneticists came to the shocking conclusion that the D.N.A. was from several different species and seemed to be impossibly fused together into the ultimate hybrid creature. The finding also scared them as this should be quite impossible using current genetic techniques. This led them, reluctantly, into the Alien theory. They proposed that only an advanced technology could account for the splicing of the D.N.A. Recent findings, however, suggest that hybrids can be made using stem cells.

I recently had a candid two-hour conversation with one of the geneticists involved in both genome studies and they told me how shocked they were and that they even considered the biblical explanation for the species where the book of Genesis describes how the fallen angels had children with human women. These offspring were called the Nephilim or the Giants. It was the working theory that whether you accept the biblical version or the ancient alien theory, they both amounted to the same thing.

I am often asked why can't we catch a Bigfoot if they are a real species? The answer is quite simple. This is a creature with a human like intelligence but possessing superhuman abilities. This a creature that has hair that allows it to perfectly blend into its surroundings. This creature can run roughly 55 miles an hour over uneven terrain. It can smell a human from a mile away and can see over a mile away. It has millions of uninhabited, forested, acres to survive and roam in around the U.S. This creature has a hinge in its foot that allows it to bend its foot at a 45-degree angle allowing for the rapid ascent of rock cliffs. A creature like that can stay secret if it chooses to and is doing just that. We have even discovered evidence of them attempting to cover up their footprints. They are smart enough to know that we notice and follow their prints.

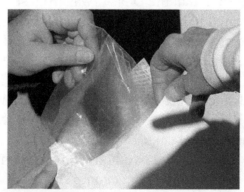

Over 1,000 hair strands collected at D.N.A. site 1.

16-inch print left at one of the D.N.A. collection sites

At some point in Earth's distant past something or someone with higher technology created this species using a myriad of D.N.A. combined with the D.N.A. of modern human women. This came as quite a shock to me, and I don't mind admitting it scared me as well. As someone who has spent an immense amount of time in the field attempting to study this species to learn that they are a genetic construct is concerning to say the least. I always thought there would be a normal biological explanation for this species but the D.N.A. proved otherwise. Add to this problem that all genetic samples are compared to the World Genetic Bank for identification. The problem with this is that only already catalogued animals are in the world gen. bank. This has led many geneticists to claim that the D.N.A. must be contaminated, unwilling or unable to imagine that such a creature can and does exist.

As if all of this weren't shocking enough the conversation turned to a phone conversation the scientist had with a colleague in the U.K. The geneticist claimed that the colleague was on his death bed and spoke about a secret genome study also undertaken by the U.K. government. He claimed that twelve different animals were captured in a remote part of Canada. Three of the individuals were caught alive. The others were not. He claimed that the results of the Top-Secret study were the same as the first genome study and that they too were shocked to find the same results. The gentleman has now passed, it is unknown at this time if he shared this information with any else.

13-inch print left at one of the D.N.A. collection sites. This print was 6-inches wide.

16 inch footprint found in the Chuska Mountains.

1 of 2 D.N.A. collection sites along with the eyewitness to the D.N.A. being left at the scene.

One of the things the Paranormal Intelligence Agency does is examine vast amounts of data pertaining to ongoing paranormal happenings. This includes a very large number of videos every week. One of the videos we analyzed frame by frame, held one of the most amazing discoveries we have ever come across. The video was shot as a hiking tutorial for the High Falls Trail in North Carolina. The gentleman who shot the video never had any idea of what he captured on film and was quite amazed after we posted a link and time stamp to his video for my readers to investigate themselves. His video began to receive hundreds of hits whereas before it had only a few dozen. He quickly removed the video wandering what was going on but now the video has been reposted. The creature he caught on film that day only appears for 3 seconds, but they could be the most important 3 seconds of film in all of cryptozoology. As we analyzed the video, we slowed it down and examined it frame by frame. At 28:53 in the film at a magnification of 600%, the clearest face of a Sasquatch ever captured was revealed. The difficulty of discovering the creature in the film and the short duration of it in the film combined with the fact that the man who shot the film never even knew he had caught this creature on film.

One of our Facebook followers mentioned that they were watching the tutorial to go on that same hike and noticed strange movement in a few frames. The following images were taken from the frames between 28 minutes and 53 seconds and 28 minutes and 56 seconds.

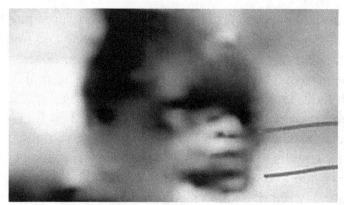

Notice the cone shaped head. Also, the facial bone structure is quite different than Homo Sapiens.

Notice how well the creature blends into its surroundings.

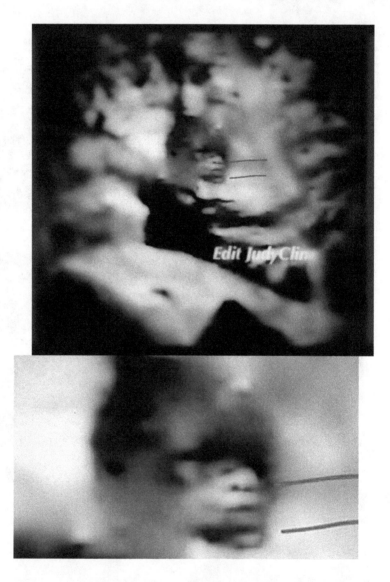

This is the same image with the blue light filtered out. The face becomes shockingly clear.

The creature possesses a cone shaped skull and its lower face is very human like. A link to this film on YouTube is posted on the Paranormal Intelligence Agency website (www.paranormal-intelligence-agency.com).

In his many years of field work, my mentor J.C. Johnson, who founded Crypto 4 Corners and was my mentor for several years, documented an amazing amount of evidence on the cryptid creatures that we were investigating. One photo stands out as the most amazing ever captured. The area where the photo was shot is still a closely held secret as operations are on-going in the area.

The Sasquatch that J.C. filmed and photographed that day is of such gargantuan size that it is jaw dropping. The creature responded to distress calls being broadcasted over portable speakers. The distress calls were recorded of what was believed to be a juvenile sasquatch from a field operation years earlier. This Sasquatch came up over a hill and then sat on a large boulder overlooking the valley where he heard the calls being broadcasted. The following photographs are of that creature.

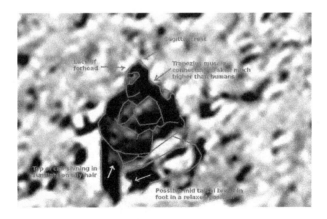

This is a still frame capture of the same exact spot with and without the creature present. It is known that these creatures are also attracted to the sound of human children playing. This creature did not seem amused by the broadcasted distress calls and scanned the area for several minutes before disappearing over the ridge line behind it.

Above: initial photograph of the creature. Below: Picture of the landscape without the creature for comparison

Photograph of same spot without the creature

Maj. Ed Dames Remote Viewers Target Bigfoot

The truth of the matter, after multiple genome studies, which were inconclusive in the eyes of much of the academic community, is that no amount of D.N.A. samples will ever be accepted as proof of this species without the accompanying remains from which the D.N.A. came. In the modern age of CGI and other picture altering software, no photographic or short video evidence will ever be accepted as proof of the species. That only leaves two ways in which the species can be verified and proven to exist once and for all in the minds of the public at large. The first and most preferable method is to film multiple creatures from multiple cameras and multiple angels, interacting with each other over a long period of time. The second is to acquire remains which cannot then be denied any longer by Universities whose respected professors scoff at the idea of Bigfoot.

Most people do not realize how high the stakes are when it comes to proving that the Sasquatch/Bigfoot species exists. The result will be to alter established academia and a great deal of religious beliefs forever. There are also indications from several disparate sources that there have been black budget efforts to somehow militarize these creatures. The public at large will fall into shock and awe over the final discovery and all those missing persons cases so eloquently researched by David Paulides in the Missing 411 books will come to forefront of public speculation. After all, when you tell the people, with undeniable proof, that a previously unknown, academically unaccepted, and ridiculed bipedal apex predator, is roaming the wilds of North America then you will alter the faith they have in the accepted version of reality as it is currently presented by modern science. This will lead to changes in our society that we cannot even fathom presently. After years of research in the field, I know that these creatures exist. I also know that the clock is ticking, and everyday technology creeps a little closer, sneaking up behind these creatures and all those other creatures which are believed not to exist.

The day is quickly approaching when undeniable proof is finally obtained. Those professors who have poured ridicule on this subject for decades despite vast amounts of physical evidence and eyewitness testimony will have to face the wrath of the public.

There is one way to greatly increase your probability of having an experience with this species. A pattern emerged a few years ago by some scientists who plotted all the known bigfoot sightings in Colorado and the dates on which the sightings occurred. They then overlaid a map of the migration pattern of the deer and elk herds. What they discovered was that the sightings followed almost exactly the pattern of the migrating deer and elk. In the Summer months, when the herds migrate back up to the high country then Bigfoot sightings occur at those altitudes. When the herds migrate back down into the lowlands during the winter to find vegetation to feed on, then Bigfoot sightings occur in the lowlands. In other words, they follow their food source and if you want to have an encounter then study the migration patterns and camp near wild herds of elk and deer.

In the South, these creatures use creeks and rivers like highways, your best bet for an encounter is to camp in the river bottoms in southeastern Oklahoma and the border area into Arkansas. A note of caution, many people think they want to have an encounter with this species till it happens. The biological response is both immediate and uncontrollable. It is pure panic filled with gut wrenching fear. At the very least, this species is perfectly evolved and adapted to its environment. It is the true master of the forest and if you have an encounter, it will change your life forever.

The implications of the public finally accepting the reality of a breeding sasquatch creatures breeding in the forests of North American are far greater than most would suppose. When the spotted all in Washington state was found to be endangered, it bankrupted the timber industry over night. You can just imagine then, what the economic repercussions will be, when it is finally proven that a species of half human creatures is living in the wilds of America. The national Park Service will be overrun with concerned parents who will be terrified to go on summer vacation to any park. All those strange disappearances of people in Americas national parks will haunt both the public and their elected officials.

This is only the beginning, the effect on the faith in established academia of our country's universities, and a great deal of religious beliefs will be to profoundly change them forever. Bigfoot lives in our collective psyche like no other cryptid creature or unsolved mystery. Mankind has always been afraid of what lurks in the dark and now it is posed to know the reason why.

Chapter 8

The Antarctica Enigma

Those who investigate such matters know that Antarctica has been the subject of much speculation of late. There have been countless trips by the power elite of the world to the south pole in recent months including Secretary of State John Kerry on election day, a day he knew no one would notice. Among these visits, the world-famous astronaut Buzz Aldrin also traveled to Antarctica only to be airlifted from the continent when health issues ensued. Besides these two notaries, a parade of world leaders and scientists have recently made trips unexpectedly to the south pole. In main stream media there are only hints as to why Antarctica is suddenly receiving such valued attention. I have been undertaking an in-depth analysis and investigation into the matter and we have assembled many pieces of the puzzle that when put together, present a breathtaking whole.

Those readers who follow Clif High's Web Bot reports that utilize neurolinguistic pattern analysis in order to discover patterns now unfolding around the world will understand for a very long time now the Web Bot has been predicting something huge going on in Antarctica. The fact is that so much information has been generated with the use of this technology that Clif has been somewhat overwhelmed by it. The reports indicate that a huge discovery has been made in Antarctica and that this discovery will have permanent and long-lasting implications for our society and the worldwide economy.

Inside sources at the P.I.A. have confirmed to us that this new discovery involves Pyramids of a very large scale. This discovery also includes what are being called pre-Adamite ruins of ancient cities which are buried 1 mile below the ice and have in recent years undergone extensive excavations. These pre-Adamite people are the Atlanteans of historical lore and many bodies have been discovered inside the ruins which are 10 to 12 feet in height and possess elongated skulls. The power elite have been prepping our society to accept such news and have made efforts recently to begin disclosure through the release of various articles in the main stream media.

Photograph of one of the pyramids in Antarctica

What is even more fascinating is that sources claim that there was an ancient intact power source also discovered within these pyramidal structures. This power source is currently not understood by modern science, but insiders claim that it will change our world forever. The P.I.A. specializes in finding patterns between sources and stories that are currently not recognized or remain unknown to researchers and the public at large. In recent years stretching back to 2012, the world renowned researcher and award winning journalist Linda Moultan Howe of Earthfiles.com has been approached by 3 separate individuals with military ties who claim that a pyramid known as the 'Dark Pyramid' or 'Black Pyramid' was discovered in Alaska. These contacts relayed an amazing amount of detail on the discovery of the 'Dark Pyramid' which is said to have been discovered in the late 1950's and at a depth of 700 feet below the surface. It is in the testimony of these individuals that we find clues as to what this power source is and more importantly how it might work.

What we know from military insiders is that the 'Dark Pyramid' is located approximately 50 miles North East of Mt. Mckinley and that the google map coordinates are 63 degrees, 18 min North; 152 degrees, 32 min West. The pyramids dimensions are 1510 feet on each side which is exactly double the dimensions of the Great pyramid at Giza which are exactly 755 ft. on each side thus the 'Dark Pyramid' is exactly 4 X the area of the base of the Great Pyramid at Giza.

Beyond this, we know that the pyramid creates fractals that efficiently distribute and multiply the power of the Earth's natural energy field. It accomplishes this because of its very strange angular orientation of 48 degrees instead of the expected orientation of 45 degrees as found in some pyramids on the earth's surface. This is related the discoveries of Nicholas Tesla who also discovered the use of fractals in his work.

Beyond these shocking revelations are the many satellite images coming from Antarctica which show entrances to these underground ruins as well as what appears to be several anomalous images of what clearly shows E.T. craft now embedded in the ancient ice of Antarctica. Researchers can find these images in the recent films that have been released by the Secure Team 10 group. The world is about to go into total shock over what is about to be released concerning Antarctica. If all the pieces fit together then the picture being formed is one that will change human history and our world forever.

Artist rendition of the black pyramid in Alaska

Our paranormal planet might me quite unique. The earth might just have the right geological make up to allow for interdimensional travel. There is an overwhelming amount of evidence for an alien presence interacting with life forms on this planet. Even hauntings are probably interdimensional bleed throughs. All paranormal activity from hauntings to cryptid animals to U.F.O.'s can be explained by my unified theory of paranormal activity. The real question is to begin to ascertain what impact these phenomena are having on this planet, and how do we as a species come to understand the implications. My quest continues, the monsters are out there, somewhere, lurking in the shadows just beyond the edge of town. Every time I strap on my gear and step into the dark woods, the following words from one of my favorite films haunts my mind.

"Once more into the fray, into the last good fight I'll ever know. Live and die on this day, live and die on this day."
-The Grey

"We are part of a symbiotic relationship with something which disguises itself as an extraterrestrial invasion so as not to alarm us."

- Terrance McKenna

9 780359 604708